Poetry Today

Poetry Today

A Critical Guide to British Poetry
1960-1984

Anthony Thwaite

Longman (London and New York)

In association with
The British Council

LONGMAN GROUP LIMITED
Longman House, Burnt Mill, Harlow
Essex CM20 2JE , England
Associated companies throughout the world

Published in the United States of America
by Longman Inc., New York
© The British Council 1985

First published 1985

BRITISH LIBRARY CATALOGUING IN PUBLICATION DATA

Thwaite, Anthony
    Poetry today: a critical guide to British poetry, 1960–1984.
    1. English poetry——20th century——History and criticism
    I. Title
    821'.914'09   PR 601
    ISBN 0-582-49419-2

LIBRARY OF CONGRESS CATALOGING IN PUBLICATION DATA

Thwaite, Anthony.
    Poetry today.

    Rev. ed. of: Poetry today, 1960–1973. 1973
    Bibliography: p.
    Includes index.
    1. English poetry——20th century——History and criticism. I. Thwaite, Anthony. Poetry today, 1960–1984. II. British Council. III. Title.
PR611. T484 1985   821'.91409   84-17114
ISBN 0-582-49419-2 (pbk)

Set in 10/12pt Linoterm Bembo
Produced by Longman Group (F.E.) Ltd
Printed in Hong Kong

Contents

List of Illustrations   vii

Prefatory Note   ix

Acknowledgements   xi

1 Poetry today   1

2 Robert Graves and David Jones   3

3 John Betjeman and William Plomer   7

4 W.H. Auden, Louis MacNeice, C. Day Lewis, Stephen Spender   12

5 George Barker, David Gascoyne, W.S. Graham, Lawrence Durrell, Norman Nicholson   22

6 Stevie Smith, Geoffrey Grigson, Roy Fuller, R.S. Thomas, Gavin Ewart, Charles Causley   25

7 'The Movement' and after:
Philip Larkin, Kingsley Amis, Robert Conquest, Elizabeth Jennings, D.J. Enright, John Wain, Donald Davie, Thom Gunn   38

8 Vernon Scannell, Dannie Abse, Patricia Beer, Laurence Lerner, John Fuller, Clive James   52

9 Ted Hughes and Sylvia Plath   56

10 'The 'Group' and after:
Peter Porter, George MacBeth, Peter Redgrove, Alan Brownjohn, Edwin Brock, Fleur Adcock, Jenny Joseph   66

11 Freda Downie, U.A. Fanthorpe, Elma Mitchell, Vicki Feaver, Carol Rumens, E.J. Scovell   78

12 Geoffrey Hill, Jon Silkin, Charles Tomlinson, Basil Bunting, Roy Fisher   82

13 'Concrete', 'Sound', 'Found':
Edwin Morgan, Bob Cobbing   93

14 'the Review' and after:
Ian Hamilton, A. Alvarez, Hugo Williams, David Harsent   97

15 'Pop' and after: 100
   Christopher Logue, Adrian Mitchell, Adrian Henri,
   Roger McGough, Brian Patten, Pete Morgan

16 Scotland, Wales, Ireland 104

17 Tony Harrison and Douglas Dunn 118

18 New poets since 1970: 123
   James Fenton, Craig Raine, Christopher Reid, Kit
   Wright, Peter Reading, John Whitworth, Peter Scupham,
   John Mole, George Szirtes, Andrew Motion, Michael
   Hulse

19 'The Poetry Business' 130

   Select Bibliography 133

   Index 144

List of Illustrations

Robert Graves	xiv
John Betjeman	8
Stevie Smith	27
R.S. Thomas	33
Philip Larkin	39
Ted Hughes	57
Geoffrey Hill	83
Seamus Heaney	113
Tony Harrison	119
James Fenton	125

Prefatory Note

The present survey is a revised and expanded version of one which the British Council commissioned well over ten years ago, and which was published as *Poetry Today 1960-1973*. If, as Harold Wilson put it, 'a week is a long time in politics', ten years in poetry can be seen as an age or a mere moment, depending on one's perspective. I have, quite naturally, made least revision to those parts of the survey in which reputations seem secure and when little or no new work has appeared: Robert Graves, David Jones, Sir John Betjeman, W.H. Auden, etc. Other important poets have needed some expansion, and sometimes extensive rewriting: R.S. Thomas, Philip Larkin, Thom Gunn, Ted Hughes, Peter Porter, George MacBeth, Geoffrey Hill, Seamus Heaney, and several others. I have added some mention of a number of new poets who have more recently come into prominence, as well as here and there reducing earlier treatment, omitting a few names. The bibliography, which many people found useful, has of course been brought up to date; but it can now be augmented with the excellent *Arts Council Poetry Library Catalogue* (1981), the most comprehensive of its kind.

As before, I have to say to readers who may be irritated by finding certain descriptions and remarks in the present essay verbally reminiscent of something they have read elsewhere that I have again not hesitated to self-plagiarize from reviews, articles and critical commentaries I have published in various places during the past ten years.

Anthony Thwaite

Acknowledgements

Thanks are due to the following publishers, authors and literary agents for permission to quote from works in copyright:

Allison & Busby Ltd: Adrian Mitchell *Adrian Mitchell's Collected Poems 1953-79, For Beauty Douglas*.

Jonathan Cape Ltd: Kingsley Amis *A Look Round the Estate*; the Executors of the Estate of C. Day Lewis *The Gate, Pegasus*; Adrian Mitchell *Ride the Nightmare*; the Estate of William Plomer *Taste and Remember*; Ted Walker *The Solitaries*.

Harry Chambers/Peterloo Poets and Elma Mitchell: Elma Mitchell *The Poor Man in the Flesh*.

Bob Cobbing: *Sound Poems: An ABC in Sound*.

Rex Collings Ltd: Tony Harrison *The School of Eloquence, Continuous*.

André Deutsch Ltd: Roy Fuller *Bluff, New Poems*.

The Dolmen Press Ltd: Thomas Kinsella *Nightwalker*.

Edinburgh University Press: Edwin Morgan *The Second Life*.

Faber & Faber Ltd: W.H. Auden *Collected Poems*; Douglas Dunn *Terry Street, St Kilda's Parliament*; Thom Gunn *Jack Straw's Castle, Moly*; Ian Hamilton *The Visit*; Seamus Heaney *North*; Ted Hughes *Crow, Wodwo*; David Jones *The Sleeping Lord*; Philip Larkin *High Windows*; Louis MacNeice *The Collected Poems of Louis MacNeice*; Paul Muldoon *Why Brownlee Left*.

Farrar, Straus & Giroux Inc. (USA): Thom Gunn *Moly, My Sad Captains, Jack Straw's Castle*; Seamus Heaney *Poems 1965–1975, Field Work*; Philip Larkin *High Windows*.

Victor Gollancz Ltd: Michael Longley *An Exploded View*; Ian Crichton Smith *Love Poems and Elegies, Selected Poems*.

Gomer Press: John Davies *At the Edge of the Town*.

Henry Graham and Jim Mangnall 'A Faceful of Agnostic Pie' (first published in PEN Anthology *New Poems 1971-72*).

Granada Publishing Ltd: George Barker *The True Confession of George Barker*; R.S. Thomas *The Bread of Truth, Not That He Brought Flowers*.

Harcourt Brace Jovanovich Inc. (USA): Kingsley Amis *A Look Round the Estate*.

Harper & Row Publishers Inc. (USA): C. Day Lewis *Selected Poems*; Sylvia

Plath *The Collected Poems of Sylvia Plath;* Ted Hughes *Crow, New Selected Poems.*

David Higham Associates Ltd: Edwin Brock *Song of the Battery Hen, The River and the Train;* Charles Causley *Collected Poems;* Glyn Hughes *Sheep;* Elizabeth Jennings *Collected Poems;* Pete Morgan *The Spring Collection;* Norman Nicholson *Sea to the West.*

Hogarth Press Ltd: George Mackay Brown *Fisherman with Ploughs;* Norman MacCaig *Measures, A Man in My Position.*

Olwyn Hughes: Sylvia Plath *Crossing the Water.*

Hutchinson Publishing Group Ltd: Patricia Beer *Collected Poems.*

John Johnson (USA rights): George Barker *The True Confession of George Barker.*

London Magazine Editions: Gavin Ewart 'Lines of History'; Tony Harrison *The Loiners.*

Longman Group Ltd: Harold Massingham *Black Bull Guarding Apples.*

George Macbeth: *The Broken Places, Poems From Oby.*

James MacGibbon: Stevie Smith *The Collected Poems of Stevie Smith.*

Macdonald Publishers: Robert Garioch *Collected Poems.*

Macmillan (Publishers) Ltd: Geoffrey Grigson *Ingestion of Ice Cream, A Skull in Salop;* R.S. Thomas *Laboratories of the Spirit;* David Wevill *Birth of a Shark.*

John Murray (Publishers) Ltd: John Betjeman *Collected Poems.*

Oxford University Press: Basil Bunting *Collected Poems;* Roy Fisher *Poems 1955–1980;* Derek Mahon *Poems 1962–1978;* Peter Porter *Preaching to the Converted, After Martial, The Last of England;* Craig Raine *A Martian Sends a Postcard Home;* Christopher Reid *Arcadia;* Charles Tomlinson *American Scenes and Other Poems.*

A.D. Peters & Company Ltd: Clive James *Fan-Mail.*

Peter Porter: *A Porter Folio.*

Random House Inc. (USA): W.H. Auden *Collected Poems* edited by Edward Mendelson; Stephen Spender *The Generous Days.*

Routledge & Kegan Paul Ltd: Donald Davie *Events and Wisdoms, Essex Poems;* Peter Redgrove *Dr Faust's Sea-Spiral Spirit;* Jon Silkin *Nature With Man.*

Salamander Press: James Fenton *Terminal Moraine*.

Secker & Warburg Ltd: Edwin Brock *Song of the Battery Hen*, *The River and the Train*; Alan Brownjohn *A Night in the Gazebo*; Freda Downie *Plainsong*; Vicki Feaver *Close Relatives*; James Fenton *Terminal Moraine*; John Fuller *Lies and Secrets*; Laurence Lerner *The Man I Killed*; Michael Longley *The Echo Gate*; George MacBeth *Poems from Oby*; John Mole *Feeding the Lade*; Pete Morgan *The Spring Collection*; Carol Rumens *Unplayed Music*; E.J. Scovell *The Space Between*.

Anthony Shiel Associates: Dannie Abse *A Small Desperation*.

University of Queensland Press: A. Alvarez *Apparition*.

Watson, Little Ltd and Chatto & Windus: D.J. Enright *Paradise Illustrated*.

A.P. Watt Ltd: Robert Graves *Collected Poems*.

Robert Graves
(Photograph Tim Motion)

1

Poetry today

In the original version of this survey, published early in 1973, I began by making much of 'the underground', 'pop poetry', 'protest poetry' and the like, as what seemed to be a vocal movement in Britain which had what I called 'its first concerted breakthrough, at the massive Albert Hall reading in 1965. Whatever view one took of such phenomena – and I was inclined to be resistant to them, as something which had more to do with show business than poetry – they were signs of an exuberant and largely young breakthrough which had been unforeseeable in, say, 1955.

Writing now in 1984, I find myself taking a historical view. To teenagers in the mid-1980s, such figures as Michael Horovitz (one of the organizers of the Albert Hall event), Adrian Henri, Roger McGough and Brian Patten are seen as seasoned performers, almost elder statesmen of entertainment – and not only of entertainment but of 'education'; for some of them have been taught in schools and enthused about by teachers with supposedly progressive notions. They have, in other words, become respectable, and are often bracketed with such comfortable zanies of the television screen as Pam Ayres and Spike Milligan, who make no pretensions whatsoever about being 'poets'.

Protest in the 1980s has a fiercer edge to it, and its exponents would certainly (but for other reasons than Pam Ayres and Spike Milligan) despise any notion of their being considered 'poets'. Such people as John Cooper Clark, Linton Kwesi Johnson, and the marvellously pseudonymous 'Attila the Stockbroker' (John Baines) tend to call what they write and recite 'rants' – ferociously anarchic doggerel, laced with obscenities and often needing a violently aggressive and amplified musical backing. So it is not prissy and superior to ignore them, having registered that they exist and sometimes have very large audiences: it is to take them at their own valuation.

As I said in the preface to the earlier version, 'The poets who had emerged and developed during the preceding decades weren't swept away and drowned by the changes in the 1960s'. There is still continuity and diversity. There is still an audience, by no means negligible, which is prepared to listen to poetry as an activity as normal and enjoyable as listening to music; and one result of the 1960s 'boom' which continues has been the recognition of this not only by the BBC (which broadcasts a good deal of new poetry on the Radio 3 network, as well as some on Radio 4) but through the very active National Poetry Secretariat (which acts as agent for organizations wanting poetry readings by poets) and the 'Writers in Schools' and 'Writers in the Community' schemes organized and funded by the Arts Council of Great Britain and by the regional arts councils. In the final section of this survey, I touch on some of the economic shrinkages and depressions of recent years, and the ways in which they have affected the publishing of poetry. But whatever the economic exigencies of the moment, or the average Englishman's embarrassment or stupefaction at mention of the words 'poet', 'poem' or 'poetry', there is no doubt that it is still a vigorous and varied art in Britain, not a dying craft which would disappear entirely without injections of patronage or money.

2

Robert Graves and David Jones

Of all the poets of a pre-1900 generation, only Robert Graves survives. T.S. Eliot died in 1965 and Edith Sitwell in 1964; both had been poetically silent for years. But while Eliot's poems are probably as much read today as ever, and while he still seems the entirely dominant figure in twentieth-century poetry in the English language, most of Edith Sitwell's work has suffered badly at the hands of time. Her *Façade* sequence is still heard in the concert hall and on records, but one feels more for the sake of William Walton's music than for her verses, sprightly though they are. Her more seriously intended poems are seldom republished or talked about.

But Graves – born as long ago as 1895 – has not only reached the fame and status of Grand Old Man but until recently was writing and publishing poems of a sharpness, tenderness, or quizzical waywardness as fresh as many he wrote years ago. He enjoys a wry sense of survival. In a sardonic squib, he quotes (or pretends to quote) from a New York review:

> Robert Graves, the British Veteran, is no longer in the poetic swim. He still resorts to traditional metres and rhyme, and to such outdated words as *tilth;* withholding his 100% approbation also from contemporary poems that favour sexual freedom.

The poem 'Tilth'★ to which this is the epigraph runs:

> Gone are the sad monosyllabic days
> When 'agricultural labour' still was *tilth;*
> And '100% approbation', *praise;*
> And 'pornographic modernism', *filth* –
> And still I stand by *tilth* and *filth* and *praise.*

★Most of the quotations from poems reproduced in this survey are extracts. Unabridged poems are indicated by an asterisk.

The mock embattled stance of a man who works to simple, classic rules is a genuine one: the poems are stylish, subdued, deeply romantic in feeling but laconic in expression, with a courtliness of address which has become the characteristic tone of later Graves: in 'Dance of Words'*, for example:

> To make them move, you should start from lightning
> And not forecast the rhythm: rely on chance,
> Or so-called chance, for its bright emergence
> Once lightning interpenetrates the dance.
>
> Grant them their own traditional steps and postures
> But see they dance it out again and again
> Until only lightning is left to puzzle over –
> The choreography plain, and the theme plain.

Many of Graves's later poems have been love poems, in which the object has often seemed to be an amalgam of a younger woman adored by an old man, the 'immanent Goddess' or muse to whom he has long professed allegiance, and a figure or figures out of distant but still passionate memory. The last is most prominent in 'A Dream of Frances Speedwell'*, but elements of all three are present:

> I fell in love at my first evening party.
> You were tall and fair, just seventeen perhaps,
> Talking to my two sisters. I kept silent,
> And never since have loved a tall fair girl,
> Until last night in the small windy hours
> When, floating up an unfamiliar staircase
> And into someone's bedroom, there I found her
> Posted beside the window in half-light
> Wearing that same white dress with lacy sleeves.
> She beckoned. I came closer. We embraced
> Inseparably until the dream faded.
> Her eyes shone clear and blue . . .
>
> Who was it, though, impersonated you?

The delicate poise and unshowy craftsmanship of Graves's poems have been respected by very many poets who show little trace of such things in their own work. Other poets have seemed to ventriloquize, adopting – as, for example, James Reeves, Kingsley Amis and Alan Brownjohn have occasionally done – that scrupulous, terse decorum with which to manage recalcitrant and subtle themes. But Graves has always been too individual, even isolated, to have had a keen following of dogmatic disciples. For years, his copious production has provided no startling shocks or disconcerting shifts, but everything has aimed towards a total unified body of work, exemplified in the fact that each individual volume has been divided into parts numbered as supplements to each successive *Collected Poems*. When a volume of *Complete Poems* is eventually published, it will show an intentness of concern remarkable for variety within unity. The contention that Graves is not only prolific but repetitive is a serious one, yet it must accept or reject Graves's own contention that to the poet there is only 'one story'. If it accepts it, it must accept what seems to be repetitiveness too; if rejected, it must look elsewhere for reasons with which to account for the distinctiveness of Robert Graves's contribution to the poetry of the century.

A much more enigmatic member of this pre-1900 generation – those who were already adults at the time of the First World War – was David Jones, poet, painter and graphic artist, whose literary work and personality were as individual as those of Graves but who has attracted a cult-following rather than general affection and admiration. Jones was a 'difficult' writer in a way that Graves never is. Whereas Graves's interest in history, mythology and religion has usually expressed itself in prose auxiliary to his verse (of a learned, capriciously scholarly, frequently polemical sort), Jones's involvement with the same subjects went directly into his creative work – *In Parenthesis, The Anathemata*, more recently *The Tribune's Visitation* and other more fragmentary pieces. The excitement to be gained from David Jones is of a kind that comes from a strange hinterland where eccentric scholarship, exalted code-cracking and the visionary gleam meet and merge. The setting of many of his later fragments is Palestine in the first century AD. The 'characters' are Roman soldiers, but – as was true of the Roman army itself – these include Celts and Greeks as well as native Romans. Thus a great deal of Celtic and Greek mythology underlies the highly allusive texture of the work, together with those incidents and phrases from modern war and soldiering which were such an integral part of *In Parenthesis*.

There are many contrasts in David Jones's poetry – between innocence and experience, between archaism and modernism, between a tenuous romantic mysticism and a hard precision of language. Underneath them all lies a preoccupation with the continuity of the Christian faith, seen in different guises and in different perspectives, sometimes underlying primitive ritual, sometimes shadowed in the Arthurian legends, often approached through its central mystery of the Mass:

> for all are members
> of the Strider's body.
> And if not of one hope
> then of one necessity.
> For we all are attested to one calling
> not any more several, but one.
> And one to what purpose?
> and by what necessity?
>
> See! I break this barrack bread, I drink with you, this
> issue cup, I salute, with you, these mutilated signa, I
> with you have cried with all of us the ratifying formula:
> *Idem in me!*
> So, if the same oath serve
> why, let the same illusions fall away.
>
> *(The Tribune's Visitation)*

In a sense, Jones seems to have attempted an historical Christian counterpart to what Ezra Pound failed to achieve, in my opinion, in the *Cantos* – a view of the flood of the past and the way in which it forces itself into the dry channels of the present. Jones's conviction of a divine transfiguring unifies his fragments in a way impossible to Pound's secular notions of 'good government'. The achievement is puzzling and not always apparently coherent, but it is an impressive achievement all the same.

3

John Betjeman and William Plomer

The appointment of Sir John Betjeman as Poet Laureate towards the end of 1972 was greeted in many quarters with the sort of good-hearted but amused condescension that one imagines might have met the announcement that Dickens's Cheeryble brothers had been invited to join the Cabinet. Betjeman's own presentation of himself, on television and in interviews, as a bumbling, untidy, genial, cranky, harmless old buffer has a great deal to do with this, and also the fact that his public preoccupations seem to have narrowed down to antiquarian preservationism and the championing of Victorian verse. In addition, there is the fact that his best known poems, such as 'A Subaltern's Love-song' ('Miss Joan Hunter Dunn, Miss Joan Hunter Dunn'), are gently absurd essays in light verse.

But there is an altogether more astringent side to Betjeman, in which nostalgia, fear, terror, hard-won faith and simple goodness contend, and a feline ferocity that is sometimes startling. The easy surfaces, lyrical measures or ambling pedestrianism of his poetry move about areas of experience which are not simple at all, and which had no proper voice until he gave them one: as much as Eliot, he has by now created the taste by which he is enjoyed. Of course he is not an innovatory and influential figure on the scale of Eliot, but his short-range colonizing of traditional areas – his awareness of the Tradition, in fact – can be seen as quite as original and striking as Eliot's grander imperialism.

Summoned by Bells (1960), the verse autobiography which takes him from childhood to going down dimly and regretfully from Oxford, has been his most sustained effort so far, though he has published many attractive shorter poems since. Written mainly in correct but conversational blank verse, interspersed with the hymn-like rhyming stanzas he has often used elsewhere, *Summoned by Bells* is full of what Betjeman himself has called 'rapid changes of mood and subject', so that it comprehends a whole complex growing personality, lightly, gravely, accurately:

John Betjeman
(Photograph Mark Gerson)

Atlantic rollers bursting in my ears,
And pealing church-bells and the puff of trains,
The sight of sailing clouds, the smell of grass –
Were always calling out to me for words.
I caught at them and missed and missed again.
'Catch hold', my father said, 'catch hold like this!',
Trying to teach me how to carpenter,
'Not *that* way, boy! When will you ever learn?' –
I dug the chisel deep into my hand.
'Shoot!' said my father, helping with my gun
And aiming at the rabbit – 'Quick, boy, fire!'
But I had not released the safety-catch.

I was a poet. That was why I failed.
My faith in this chimera brought an end
To all my father's hopes. In later years,
Now old and ill, he asked me once again
To carry on the firm, I still refused.
And now when I behold, fresh-published, new,
A further volume of my verse, I see
His kind grey eyes look woundedly at mine,
I see his workmen seeking other jobs,
And that red granite obelisk that marks
The family grave in Highgate Cemetery
Points an accusing finger at the sky.

Betjeman's *Collected Poems* (several times revised and added to since its first publication in 1958: the 1979 edition is the latest) and its successors continue to have both a popular and a critical success, and by no means appeal exclusively to the 'upper-middle-class and lower-middle-aged' public characterized as such by a derogatory commentator. Both Auden and Larkin have praised him, and one can see why: Auden recognized the versatile technical skill, Larkin the 'dramatic urgency' that springs from 'what he really feels about real life'. The urgency is part of the skill, speaking nakedly but with decorum from a basic melancholy, as in 'NW5 & N6'. In this poem, the careful and circumstantial re-creation of childhood, of a sadistic nurse imposing her puritan will in the midst of outwardly cosy suburbia, moves to its blank and bleak conclusion:

> 'World without end'. It was not what she'ld do
> That frightened me so much as did her fear
> And guilt at endlessness. I caught them too,
> Hating to think of sphere succeeding sphere
> Into eternity and God's dread will
> I caught her terror then. I have it still.

William Plomer was often paired with John Betjeman, and it is true that both emerged in the early 1930s as satirists and writers of light verse. Plomer went on to develop his own brand of 'sick' humour, most outrageously and memorably in such poems of the 1940s as 'The Dorking Thigh', 'The Flying Bum' and 'The Self-Made Blonde'. All these are exercises in straight-faced shock, and the urbane mockery rides easily over the gruesome nastiness of the incidents described. In them, Plomer toyed elegantly with the bizarre, using brisk and breezy stanzas and jaunty rhymes. In his later work there was much less concern with satire and absurdity. Pathos and wistfulness seemed to have taken over, in such poems as 'Lime-Flower Tea', in which an old man walks the esplanade of a seaside town before returning to his 'neurotic childless wife':

> His walk alone at night she understands
>   And the unsaid;
> In the warm room she'll pour out,
>   Before bed,
> Delicately, lime-flower tea;
>   Together they will sip and dream,
> Sad and content, both drugged
>   By the lost summer in the scented steam.

This is one of the fragile successes of *Taste and Remember,* the volume from which it comes; but it is a mark of one's old expectations that at a first reading the poem seems to be poised for some horrific conclusion – the man killing his wife with arsenic in that lime-flower tea, or strangling her with his old school tie. The thought is unworthy, but it is difficult to escape the conviction that the gravity, thoughtfulness and sincerity of Plomer's later poems have a heaviness of language and movement which, together with an emotional obviousness, lack the distinction of his former shockers.

4

W.H. Auden, Louis MacNeice, C. Day Lewis, Stephen Spender

The old quadrumvirate of the 1930s, lampooned into mythical unity by Roy Campbell as 'MacSpaunday', has long since disintegrated. Auden continues to be the commanding figure, even after his death in 1973. Louis MacNeice died in 1963, C. Day Lewis in 1972. Since his *Collected Poems* of 1955, Stephen Spender has published only one volume of verse, *The Generous Days* (1971). True, there is a continued interest in the poets and poetry of that pre-war decade, shown rather oddly in Robin Skelton's Penguin *Poetry of the 1930s* and more adventurously in the special 'Thirties' number of *the Review* which appeared in 1964. Yet as Auden said, he published more poetry since that decade than during it, and the same could be said of MacNeice, Day Lewis and Spender.

There are some who hold to a persuasion (loyal but aggrieved, given to disappointment rather than condemnation) that W.H. Auden's importance as a poet began to diminish rapidly and disastrously with his departure to America not long before the Second World War. Such people instance prolixity where there used to be terseness, smugness where there was unease, cosy verbal games in place of urgent and memorable warnings. But the decade of the 1930s – in the English-speaking world of poetry so much the Age of Auden – is not a period to be prolonged out of feelings of nostalgia, whether genuine or vicarious; the *Poems* (1930) still survive, and *The Orators,* and all the rest of the pre-1941 work, whatever Auden did or didn't do to it in the way of revision or suppression. It is an assembly of work that embodies a period in the way that much good poetry does, but we should not expect Auden in his sixties to perpetuate – by imitation, as it were – the Auden of his twenties and thirties. He became a sage rather than a prophet; but above all he was still supremely an entertainer, a virtuoso who believed that poetry can display many voices, many skills, and that it has something to do with the disinterested intelligence:

>   After all, it's rather a privilege
>   amid the affluent traffic
> to serve this unpopular art which cannot be turned into
>   background noise for study
> or hung as a status trophy by rising executives,
>   cannot be 'done' like Venice
> or abridged like Tolstoy, but stubbornly still insists upon
>   being read or ignored: our handful
> of clients at least can rune.
>
>   ('The Cave of Making')

I think it is worth noting that younger poets (such as John Fuller and James Fenton) who have responded sympathetically and affectionately to Auden during these past few years have done so with particular attention to the post-war poetry – *Nones, Homage to Clio, About the House,* and so on. Auden is still a force, not a spent one.

About the House (1966) is the first of the Auden books to fall within the period of this essay, and it had three serious successors, *City Without Walls* (1969), *Epistle to a Godson* (1972) and *Thank You, Fog* (1974): *Academic Graffiti* (1971) can be bracketed off as the entertainer indulging himself with games that could be properly characterized as cosy, unashamedly minor, and often not very successful even on their own terms. The Auden of the other books is someone who gratefully found a way of life and a place in which to live it: the twelve poems in 'Thanksgiving for a Habitat' (from *About the House*) in particular celebrated his 'toft-and-croft' in Austria, a haven of routine and mild pleasure among his 'own little Anglo-American musico-literary set'. Tetchily content, unconvinced and repelled by the cant of the young and the politically zealous, he frequently looked back to his childhood (a privileged one of nannies and Greek, antique symbols now) and contrasted it with the uncomely present of

>   lasers, electric brains,
>   do-it-yourself sex manuals,

bugged phones, sophisticated
weapon-systems and sick jokes.

('Prologue at Sixty')

Privacy and common sense, friendship and good manners, the
blessing of survival itself – these are the daily benefits for which he
was thankful. But this *otium liberale,* this cultured retirement, is
given its special edge through Auden's peculiar technical gifts, by
which the commonplace is enjoyed in a thoroughly uncommonplace
vocabulary, erudite, quirky, and often donnishly eccentric:

In his dream zealous
To attain his home,
But ensorcelling powers
Have contorted space,
Odded the way;
Instead of a facile
Five-minute trot,
Far he must hirple,
Clumsied by cold,
Buffeted often
By blouts of hail
Or pirries of rain,
On stolchy paths
Over glunch clouds,
Where infrequent shepherds,
Sloomy of face,
Smudge of spirit,
Snoachy of speech,
With scaddle dogs
Tend a few scrawny
Cag-mag sheep

('A Bad Night')

He could be grander and less neologistic than this: 'An Encounter' (which observes a meeting between 'Attila and his Hun Horde' and Pope Leo by the River Po in the year 452) needs no recourse to the Oxford English Dictionary and makes a real point about the mysteries of civilization and barbarism. He could also be delightfully straightforward and witty, as in 'On the Circuit', which considers the modern ordeal-by-culture of the peripatetic poet on a reading tour:

> An airborne instrument I sit,
> Predestined nightly to fulfil
> Columbia-Giesen-Management's
> Unfathomable will, . . .
>
> And daily, seven days a week,
> Before a local sense has jelled,
> From talking-site to talking-site
> Am jet-or-prop-propelled.

Emotional urgency and a deeply committed sense of struggle both with life and with one's material seem to be basic requirements demanded by many critics of poetry today. The fact that Auden's post-war work conspicuously lacks these, is indeed contemptuous of them, partly accounts for the way in which he has been taken at his own valuation, as a reactionary and rather supercilious mandarin who looked back to a time when

> . . . Speech was a mannerly, an Art
> Like learning not to belch or fart:
> I cannot settle which is worse,
> The Anti-Novel or Free Verse.
>
> ('Doggerel by a Senior Citizen')

Yet Auden's actual performance, his wide-ranging and individual experience, equally at home or not-at-home on his 'Austrian ground', as a carpet-slippered celebrator of Oxford eccentricities or as 'a New Yorker, who opens his *Times* at the obit page', belie the limitations he seems to have assigned to himself and which others have chosen to accept or condemn. 'The Cave of Making' (his memorial poem for Louis MacNeice)' 'Whitsunday in Kirchstetten', 'Prologue at Sixty', 'Old People's Home', and 'Talking to Myself' are all poems in which Auden is at the centre, ruminating, conversational, at ease with himself but without self-satisfaction, and they speak from true and deeply-felt concerns with a wisdom and decent mannerliness, aware without huffing and puffing that

Virtue is always
more expensive than Vice, but
cheaper than Madness.

('Shorts I')★

The Auden whose dramatic characters in the 1930s (according to Isherwood) were always ready to flop on their knees became less inclined to preach and prescribe, lecture and warn, and was 'Most at home with what is Real'. His later work had a different, not an inferior, validity.

When Louis MacNeice died in September 1963, he was going through a rich and extended creative phase, the evidence of which can be seen in his last two books, *Solstices* (1961) and *The Burning Perch,* which he had prepared for press and which appeared only a few days after his death. MacNeice had always been a prolific poet, but there had been periods in his life – particularly during the late 1940s and most of the 1950s – when the machine appeared to be running with not much more than fluency: his actual power had seemed to be waning in such work as *Autumn Sequel,* for example. But the last two books are a fine (and, as it turned out, final) flowering, and they contain poems as good as anything he wrote.

MacNeice has increasingly seemed to me the most immediately attractive of the MacSpaunday quartet, and at the same time a much more serious and complex figure than he has sometimes been taken to be. His upbringing as the son of a gloomy Ulster Protestant clergyman ('Between a smoking fire and a tolling bell'), his training as a classical scholar, his quiet relish of the ordinary pleasures of life tempered by a steady and stoical pessimism – all these are elements in his work, and all of them were handled with a well-judged lyrical virtuosity. More and more, a melancholy tunefulness seems the manner of his last poems:

O never force the pace, they said;
Leave it alone, you have lots of time,
Your kind of work is none the worse
For slow maturing. Do not rush.
   He took their tip, he took his time,
   And found his time and talent gone.

Oh you have had your chance, It said;
Left it alone and it was one.
Who said a watched clock never moves?
Look at it now. Your chance was I.
   He turned and saw the accusing clock
   Race like a torrent round a rock.

('The Slow Starter')

They are not in any ordinary sense the poems of a dying man, for MacNeice's death was sudden and unexpected; yet they are indeed much concerned with slow decline, extinction and nullity, watched with a jaunty and devil-may-care insouciance. Even the games he so enjoyed and celebrated in his poems serve as a text (in 'Sports Page') for the conclusion that

The lines of print are always sidelines
And all our games funeral games.

Themes of childhood, of nostalgia, are wedded to forms and metres that often have something of the nursery rhyme or the folk poem about them, and in 'Château Jackson' he builds a whole mysteriously nihilistic *tour de force* on the structure of the old verses about the house that Jack built. The idea of play is strong in MacNeice's last poems, but it is always play with a purpose and done to strict rules: this too is part of the child-world, as is the emphasis on magic, the irrational and dreams, the sense of *déjà vu* which is both exhilarating and frightening:

It does not come round in hundreds of thousands of years,
It comes round in the split of a wink, you will be sitting exactly
Where you are now and scratching your elbow, the train
Will be passing exactly as now and saying It does not come
                                                              round,
It does not come round, It does not come round, and compactly
The wheels will mark time on the rails and the bird in the air
Sit tight in its box and the same bean of coffee be ground
That is now in the mill and I know what you're going to say
For all this has happened before, we both have been through the
                                                              mill, . . .

('Déjà vu')

MacNeice's *Collected Poems,* carefully edited by E.R. Dodds and published in 1966, span a period of almost forty years and make up a very varied and substantial body of work. His poems have always been great favourites with the anthologists (I am thinking of such familiar pieces as 'Bagpipe Music', 'The sunlight on the garden', 'Prayer Before Birth' and 'Snow'), and there are several in his last two books which will I am sure go on having that sort of life: 'Soap Suds', 'Apple Blossom', 'The Truisms', and – one of the poems written at the very end of his life – 'Thalassa'. But he deserves to be read as a whole, and the *Collected Poems* make up one of the most continuously entertaining books to be published for many years.

C. Day Lewis, who died in 1972 after a long illness, was probably as prolific a writer as MacNeice, and his reputation went through as many fluctuations. After his *Collected Poems* of 1954, he published four further volumes. Many of the poems in them have a sense of being 'occasional' pieces, celebrating dead friends and dead artists, rediscovering places and roots in his native Ireland, commemorating specific moments of pleasure or pain. The manner is sweetly lyrical, gently melancholy, and the general impression is a little too bland. Throughout his poetic career, Day Lewis's chief disablement was that he seemed to respond too easily to the seductive voices of those poets he admired: Auden in his early days, and later a whole *mélange* of influences – in particular Meredith and, most of all, Hardy. His generous and genial temperament tended to soften his mentors, making them diffuse and losing their defining edges. Even such an attractive poem as 'Walking Away' (from *The Gate*, 1962) suffers from this blurring effect: in it, the poet remembers watching his young son, now a grown man, walking away from him to school 'With the pathos of a half-fledged thing set free/Into a wilderness', and the feel of the detail in these first three stanzas is Hardyesque, as is the movement of the verse. But the final stanza moralizes in a wistful way that sounds like diluted Robert Frost:

I have had worse partings, but none that so
Gnaws at my mind still. Perhaps it is roughly
Saying what God alone could perfectly show –
How selfhood begins with a walking away,
And love is proved in the letting go.

The sincerity is moving, but it lacks final authenticity because of the echoes, the uneasy awareness of high pastiche.

I think these are proper objections, not mere fussing about 'influences'. Yet the fact remains that Day Lewis's poems give a good deal of pleasure to a large number of people, who perhaps find that emotional honesty and emotional simplicity of his kind, matched with graceful and rather obviously musical cadences, override more rigorous demands. The decent commonplaces of such a poem as 'The House where I was Born' illustrate this well:

No one is left alive to tell me
In which of those rooms I was born,
Or what my mother could see, looking out one April

Morning, her agony done,
Or if there were pigeons to answer my cooings
From that tree to the left of the lawn.

The conventional judgement on Stephen Spender's work is that his early poems, in his first two books, are his best. In my opinion it is also the right judgement, and neither the *Collected Poems* of 1955 nor the single volume that has followed (*The Generous Days*, 1971) seem to countermand it. I am not thinking of such early pieces as 'I think continually of those who were truly great' or 'The Express' or 'Landscape Near an Aerodrome', all of which are familiar anthology entries, but of stumblingly eloquent and strange poems like 'Without that once clear aim', 'Not places, an era's crown', 'Two Armies' and 'Port Bou', in which cloudy but passionate states of mind are fixed and defined with sensitive strokes. After that, there seems a gradual loss of verbal conviction; the personality seems much the same, but it has lost its lonely concentration.

Something of this can be shown by quoting two of the nine stanzas of 'If It Were Not', the first poem in *The Generous Days*:

Mountain, star and flower
Single with my seeing
Would–gone from sight–draw back again
Each to its separate being.

Nor would I hoard against
The obliterating desert
Their petals of the crystal snow
Glittering on the heart.

All the key words here (mountain, star, flower, desert, petals, crystal, heart, and of course the first person pronouns) are found over and over again in the early poems; yet there they moved unexpectedly, and seemed real and necessary emblems rather than counters – as in

The promise hangs, this swarm of stars and flowers,
And then there comes the shutting of a door.

As with the later Day Lewis, much of *The Generous Days* seems prompted, without much sense of inevitability or necessity, by 'occasions'. Some of these have a rougher texture, a more spontaneous feeling of being raw material, than is usual in Spender, but the result is no fresher. 'Art Student', for example, mimes the shambling crudity of its subject but the effect is not one of impressionism but of perfunctoriness. The best poem in the book harks back to the very time when the early poems were written – in the Oxford of 'One More New Botched Beginning', where the precise detail is documentary in its effect.

5

George Barker, David Gascoyne, W.S. Graham, Lawrence Durrell, Norman Nicholson

Among the many other poets who emerged in the 1930s and 1940s (most of them born between the years 1910–20), some were killed during the Second World War or have died since, some have gone silent, a few have developed and strengthened their reputations, and some have gone on writing and publishing but without adding much of value to their earlier work. George Barker is one of the most problematical figures. At a time when his close contemporary, Dylan Thomas, was also beginning to be noticed, it was Barker, not Thomas, who was picked out by Yeats for inclusion in the *Oxford Book of Modern Verse* (1936). Francis Scarfe's book *Auden and After,* which gives a fair picture of critical orthodoxies in the early 1940s, gave equal prominence to Barker and Thomas. But since Thomas's death in 1953 there has been no doubt which of the two poets has had greater attention and praise. In the past thirty years, Barker has seemed to be judged as if he lay in the shadow of Thomas's fame.

This is a pity, because throughout his career Barker's best poems have been striking and powerful. Since 1960 he has published eight new full-length books of verse (as well as much poetry for children). Although most of them lack the unified impact of his best pre-1960 books (*Lament and Triumph,* 1940, and *Eros in Dogma,* 1944), there are magnificent things in all of them – as well as the faults of prolixity, verbal and rhythmical ludicrousness, vatic pretension and high-flown automatism that have marked much of his output from the very beginning. His most ambitious effort has been *The True Confession of George Barker,* the first part of which appeared in 1950 but which was published in its complete form in 1965. The anguished and majestic rhetoric of some of its sections is like nothing else in modern English poetry:

Not in our deep and mutual
  Need of Love can we confute
That we live in the incommunicable
  And lonely liberty of the brute:
Not there, but in the complicity
  Of moral treason, in the trust
Betrayed by the heart's duplicity,
  The marriage of our dust.

Other poems commemorate the dead or highly-charged evocative places: the painters John Minton and Robert Colquhoun, the poets MacNeice and Eliot, landscapes in Italy and England. The grandly simplified elegiac note of these is best caught in a poem in memory of his father, 'At Thurgarton Church', which takes this bare Norfolk chapel as a setting for a meditation on death:

I hear the old bone in me cry
and the dying spirit call:
I have forfeited all
and once and for all must die
and this is all that I know

Barker continues, as he has always done, to take great risks within the romantic convention of the poet as divine scapegoat, but the assured seriousness of this stance, together with his eloquent gifts, more often achieve success than he is given credit for. His long meditative poem *Anno Domini* (1983) is both quietly ironical and powerful.

David Gascoyne, who emerged precociously with his first book of poems when he was only sixteen, who pioneered Surrealism in England in the 1930s, and whose *Poems 1937–1942* was one of the best books produced during the Second World War, has published very little indeed in the years covered by this survey; but it is worth noticing that in spite of this there has been a renewed interest in his work recently, particularly among young people – part of a reassessment of and fashion for Surrealism, to some extent nurtured in the universities and colleges of art. To some, W.S. Graham (who first came to notice as part of the so-called 'New Apocalypse' in the 1940s) has become an equally interesting figure; but Graham has continued to publish, and to change. His *Malcolm Mooney's Land* (1970) spoke rather in the same riddling, mesmerized voice of old, but *Implements in Their Places* (1977), though oracular, was plainer, and his *Collected Poems 1942–1977* (1979) put him in perspective as a more interestingly developing writer than once seemed likely. Lawrence Durrell's fastidious classic-romantic flavour and his concentration on subjects that are exotic yet carefully circumstantial have a quality in his poems that is likely to outlast the flamboyance and over-elaboration of his prose fiction; though this quality is found too in his travel books, such as *Prospero's Cell* and *Bitter Lemons*. His *Collected Poems 1931–1974* (1980) shows him at his peak in the late 1930s and early 1940s, but there are a few later poems (such as 'A Patch of Dust', written in 1974) which beautifully catch the old freshness, that assured movement through a Mediterranean historical/hedonistic terrain.

Norman Nicholson's work, from its beginnings in the 1940s, has been almost totally absorbed in the landscapes, characters and ancestries of his native Cumberland, where he has always lived. It has an authenticity which has been recognized and praised in his two most recent books, *A Local Habitation* (1972) and *Sea to the West* (1981), sharing some of his fellow-Cumbrian Wordsworth's concerns without being dominated by them – as in 'On the Dismantling of Millom Ironworks':

And maybe the ghost of Wordsworth, seeing further than I can,
Will stare from Duddon Bridge, along miles of sand and mud-
                                                                    flats
To a peninsula bare as it used to be, and, beyond, to a river
Flowing, untainted now, to a bleak, depopulated shore.

6

Stevie Smith, Geoffrey Grigson, Roy Fuller, R.S. Thomas, Gavin Ewart, Charles Causley

Half a dozen poets who first published in the 1930s and 1940s have clearly survived without diminution, went on writing well during at least part of the period of this essay, and in some cases are deservedly better known now than at any time in their writing careers. In order of age (which I would admit is tidy rather than illuminating) they are Stevie Smith (who died in 1971), Geoffrey Grigson, Roy Fuller, R.S. Thomas, Gavin Ewart and Charles Causley. Each is very much an individual, though one could argue the importance of Auden – as an example or model – to Grigson, Fuller and Ewart.

Stevie Smith was a complete original. Someone once said that she was like William Blake rewritten by Ogden Nash, but though that is quite smart it doesn't really catch her unique mixture of whimsical gloom, eccentric common sense, incantation, nursery rhyme, doggerel and rhythmical subtlety. Towards the end of her life (and she spent sixty-five years of it living in the same house in an unfashionable part of north London), she wrote that she felt 'as if I were looking out through a beautiful window at a distance that is full of amiability but has cast a spell. I do not mind this, in fact rather like it.' That is very much the note of Stevie Smith's poems – a note not often heard in modern poetry. Indeed, when she first tried to publish her poems in the mid-1930s she found little enthusiasm for them. It was only gradually that she came to be recognized as a very special poet of strangeness, loneliness and quirky humour, particularly with her *Selected Poems* of 1962 and the Penguin selection published in the same year. There followed *The Frog Prince* (1966), the posthumous *Scorpion* (1972), and *Collected Poems* (1975).

Stevie Smith often made poems out of fancies and odd imaginings which might have seemed to anyone else unpromising and quite unpoetic, such as the lines:

Do take Muriel out
She is looking so glum
Do take Muriel out
All her friends have gone . . .

Do take Muriel out
Although your name is Death . . .

('Do Take Muriel Out')

She was always a poet concerned with death, and during her last
years it had been her central theme – not really gloomy, but seen in
an almost sprightly way: Death as something to be comfortably
welcomed, like a neighbour:

I have a friend
At the end
Of the world.
His name is a breath

Of fresh air.
He is dressed in
Grey chiffon. At least
I think it is chiffon.
It has a
Peculiar look, like smoke.

('Black March')

The quality of her poems was immensely enhanced by her own
reading (or often chanting or singing) of them: her readings *became*
her poems, with her inimitable blend of levity, loneliness, and
sometimes asperity. She could sustain a narrative (as in 'Angel
Boley'), indulge in sly theological polemics '(How do you see the
Holy Spirit of God?'), be bewilderingly whimsical ('Mrs Blow and
Her Animals') or quietly poignant ('Oblivion'), and her humour was
offhand and mocking:

Stevie Smith
(Photograph BBC)

The foolish poet wonders
Why so much honour
Is given to other poets
But to him
No honour is given.

('The Poet Hin')

It is fortunate that a number of recordings of her readings exist, so that her authentic and memorable manner is preserved.

The sort of pretensions Stevie Smith mocked are even more extensively and scathingly treated in some of Geoffrey Grigson's poems. When he was editor of *New Verse* in the 1930s, his activities with what he has called the 'billhook' cut down the pompous, the fatuous, the obscurantist, the careerist and the dim in large and bloody swathes. In the startingly active years that followed his *Collected Poems* of 1963 (augmented in his *Collected Poems 1963–1980*), he has been memorably contemptuous – of a *cause célèbre* involving a well-known Scottish poet, for example:

Because MacOssian thieves what other men have written
Detested bullying Englishmen abuse him.
Why not, when only reiving
Lallans-leaking Scots excuse him?

('Master of Aleatory Verse')★

Or of a literary lord who renounced his peerage:

Peers have been made whose hired robes have hidden
A depth of wallowing in the dirtiest midden.
Here was a lord – his hopes and head were both too big –
Who doffed his ermine and revealed a pig.

('On a Change of Style')★

But though these epigrams, together with snarls and brief fits of petulance against 'smart reviewers', 'Journalist-dons, hair-oiled ad-men', and the inanities of television culture, are characteristic of one side of Grigson's personality in his poetry, they are not dominant. Most of his recent poems have been sensuous notations of places, people and very closely observed scenes, celebrations of the oddity and variety of natural life. It is the passionate naturlist, archaeologist, topographer and traveller that watches from the centre of Grigson's poems, restlessly particularizing and recording: 'Let us precisely state' is a phrase from a poem in *Ingestion of Ice-Cream* (1969), and that is what he does. Of 'Old Man by a Lake in June', he observes:

> Balances – how shrunken he is. Dives, from
> ten feet, breaks reflections of mountains, swims
> with long easy strokes, arms thrusting
> ahead of his head, as if he were young, past brown
> children the town instructor is teaching to swim.

In this poem the detail is almost pedestrian, but the cumulative effect is not so. Elsewhere Grigson is sometimes finically intense, so concerned with precise shades of colour, textures, quiddities, that certain poems become static and cluttered. But his talent for enjoyment, even when it turns amiably bitter or waspish, is one that genuinely communicates a sense of the unrepeatable moment. In at least two poems he celebrates the 'quizzical classical' talent of Louis MacNeice, who himself delighted in 'the drunkenness of things being various', and MacNeice's phrase epitomizes Grigson's own quality.

Roy Fuller's poems began to appear during the 1930s, in such magazines as Grigson's *New Verse*. They had a pretty strong taste of Auden about them, and were witty, intelligent, rather dry, very much aware of what was going on in the political world round him but having a wry detachment as well. Though he went on to write better poems than these, such qualities still hold good in Fuller's work. But one began to be aware that he wasn't just a rather better-than-average 'reporter of experience' in the late 1950s, with such poems as 'The Ides of March', in which his capacity for rich and developed thinking-aloud became apparent, and a technical ability which showed itself in a whole range of forms working out a shaping and phrase-making imagination. His *Collected Poems* of 1962 have been followed by six more volumes, the best being *New Poems* (1968). This showed an even more striking development, in which his strict forms and ingenious rhymes were largely jettisoned and the voice became deceptively relaxed and low-keyed, allowing moments of blankness or self-disgust or facetiousness to be caught entirely without straining pose or frigid distancing:

> Girl with fat legs, reading Georgette Heyer,
> Shall I arrange you in my pantheon?
>
> ('Romance')

> Is it possible that anyone so silly can
> Write anything good?
>
> ('Last Sheet')

> If I became penniless tomorrow . . .
> Still impossible to change to a hero of art!
>
> ('Chinoiserie')

These quotations from three different poems show a nakedness of address risky in its fidelity. But these low and absurd self-observations modulate quite naturally and with suppleness into something graver, more elevated and eloquent: Fuller earns the right to this through plotting his progression. Thus the first quotation – a snobbish mock-rhetorical flourish – begins both by disarming one and making one prickle with embarrassment, but ends:

> Return, great goddesses, and your society
> Where even little girls develop
> Strong superegos, and the misfortune

Of woman's weak moral nature is unknown;
And the wars are waged on a lower epicycle
By armour diminutive as stag-beetles;
And poets forbidden to sing of their diseases
Or amatory botherations;
And only with end-stopped irony.

('Romance')

Without being academic, Fuller is an alert, very widely read, end-lessly curious and unashamedly intellectual poet. More than any poet since Auden, he has used his reading of Freud and Jung in trying to make sense of human drives and infirmities, and he has a strong sense of history. In his sequence of sonnets 'The Historian', Fuller's persona considers 'the notion of the Wall and Counter Wall' at Syracuse, and concludes:

I see at every crucial turn of fate
Those soldier-labourers, those citizen-
Victims at their crass, suicidal tricks;
And find, to say the least, inadequate
The rueful groans that rose on all sides when
They turned from love or art to handle bricks.

As a defender of rigorous intelligence, the maintenance of demanding standards and the hopelessness of over-generosity to the merely wet, warm or wilful. Fuller was to some extent ignored as Professor of Poetry at Oxford where many students – in common with their fellows elsewhere – were distrustful of what they regarded as arid reasonableness. But what he has casually called 'brain power allied at least to a dogged alertness and integrity' – his criterion of success in poetry – is very much his mixture, and it will survive.

The dryness of Roy Fuller's poetry, when it exists, is the dryness of analytical enquiry: in R.S. Thomas, it seems a quality of the whole personality. The books of poems he has published during the past several years have become increasingly stark, grim, resigned and laconic: the very title of one – *H'm* – a baleful brief shudder. In *The Bread of Truth* (1963), his homily 'To a Young Poet' ends:

> You are old now
> As years reckon, but in that slower
> World of the poet you are just coming
> To sad manhood, knowing the smile
> On her proud face is not for you.

The face, of course, is that of the 'cold queen' who chooses (or doesn't choose) to dispense her favours to poets. If this muse has a local habitation in Thomas's poems, it is to be found in the Welsh hill country, the dead end of rural Wales, where he worked as a priest for more than thirty years. The tenant farmers who inhabit these hills and Thomas's poems are as grim and resigned as he, working unprofitable acres. To them, nature is a cheat:

> In clear pools
> In the furrows they watch themselves grow old
> To the terrible accompaniment of the song
> Of the blackbird, that promises them love.
>
> ('Tenancies')

Although his poems are steeped in his experience of Wales, and although many of them show resentment at the invasions of cosmopolitanism, urbanism, tourism – in short, the English – Thomas's attitude to Wales and the Welsh is ambivalent, and is more so now than ever:

> Where can I go, then, from the smell
> Of decay, from the putrefying of a dead
> Nation?
>
> ('Reservoirs')

R.S. Thomas
(Photograph Universal Pictorial Press)

And the title of his poem 'Welcome to Wales' turns ironically sour
with its opening lines:

> Come to Wales
> To be buried; the undertaker
> Will arrange it for you.

Acceptance and rejection work away behind a stonily unflinching
face.

More recently Thomas has enlarged his range so that each new
poem seems to become a continuation of what he calls the
'linguistic confrontation with ultimate reality', a kind of contentious
struggling through paradox after paradox with a creator and/or
saviour who has all the odds stacked on his side. This has been
accompanied by a greater reliance on the effect of cadence and
modulation, less on the impact of metaphor or anything much in the
way of figurative language. The resultant statements are both very
plain and challengingly intense – confrontations with God or no-
God, faith or lack of faith; meditations on and arguments about
human and spiritual existence; sometimes brief parables or fables.
On the page, the breaks between the lines in these more recent
poems may seem to have no significance; but read aloud, they are
certainly not prose:

> I have seen the sun break through
> to illuminate a small field
> for a while, and gone my way
> and forgotten it. But that was the pearl
> of great price, the one field that had
> the treasure in it. I realize now
> that I must give all that I have
> to possess it. Life is not hurrying
>
> on to a receding future, nor hankering after
> an imagined past. It is the turning
> aside like Moses to the miracle

of the lit bush, to a brightness
that seemed as transitory as your youth
once, but is the eternity that awaits you.

('The Bright Field')★

Gavin Ewart's poems fall into two long-separated periods. He had a
precocious start: some of his early work appeared in *New Verse* when
he was in his teens, and his first book (*Poems and Songs,* 1938) had a
cheeky freshness, full of the lighter side of Auden – the four lines
about Miss Twye soaping her breasts in the bath have become
favourite anthology material. Then there was silence, only
sporadically interrupted, for over twenty years, until a succession of
Ewart publications began to appear in the mid-1960s. The odd thing
is that the revivified Ewart turns out to be recognizably the same as
the old, his humour blacker and more scabrous than before, perhaps,
but then we are told we live in permissive times. The formal
structures of the poems – their shapes and sizes – are dashingly
various: Ewart himself has said that 'the more technical expertise
goes into a poem, as a general rule, the more interesting it is'. He is
not primarily interested in 'importance' (certainly not if it has to be
of a solemn kind), much more in entertainment. In this area, as with
comic anecdotes, there isn't much room for approximation: the
target must be hit in the bull or not at all. Here Ewart's copiousness
sometimes fails, and he produces a number of shots that seem
literally pointless, jokes that misfire.
 But whatever the relative failures of some jokes, many are black:
'A Black Rabbit Dies For Its Country' (an observation on
experiments in chemical warfare), 'The Name of the Game' (a
fragmentary anatomizing of an advertising agency, a milieu in
which Ewart worked for many years), more lightly 'Jerzy' (an
Ogden-Nash-like look at adultery) – all these representative poems
look at what Ewart has called 'the pressures and pleasures of
contemporary urban life' with a mordant awareness of the
unpleasant ironies. There is something both attractively and
disdainfully offhand about Ewart's poems, even when they seem
inclined to be serious, as in 'Lines of History'★:

By a deserted road the Apostles were peeing.

The sun through the burning-glass tickled the warm hay.

The sea heaved with its burden of whales.

The antheap was teeming with cries of injustice.

Above the wine shop she cupped her hands and held him.

Past the window of the torture chamber flew the pigeons.

There was no silence, now or at any time.

Ewart's enormous *The Collected Ewart* (1980) is a cornucopia of his
prolific, entertaining, uneven talent. He continues to be prolific, and
his poems get funnier and funnier.

Although Charles Causley's first collection of poems was not
published until 1951, he began writing during the war when he was
in the navy, and thirty years later the sea is still often present in his
work. The sea-shanty, the ballad, the jaunty narrative have always
been his forms, outwardly simple, often humorous, always bright
and melodious. But his range has widened and deepened, and some
of his best poems are found in two of his more recent collections,
Underneath the Water and *Figure of Eight* – the second book is
published for children, but it isn't markedly different from the rest of
his work.

Causley's earlier brisk ballads sometimes seem a little too
resolutely jolly, but he isn't the simple old-fashioned lyrical soul
some people take him for. In 'Ballad of the Bread Man', for instance,
the lively step of the verse is quite clearly and deliberately working
against what it is actually saying, and the contrast is a large part of the
effect:

Mary stood in the kitchen
Baking a loaf of bread.
An angel flew in through the window.
We've a job for you, he said.

Even when the verse is reduced to something very like doggerel, as
in 'I Saw A Jolly Hunter', the effect is a sophisticated one, calling on

memories of nursery rhymes to give the poem irony. And Causley
has a grander, more measured manner too, often drawing on the
personal and circumstantial, with the old lyrical sweetness but with
new depths – at the end of 'Conducting a Children's Choir':

> I bait the snapping breath, curled claw, the deep
> And delicate tongue that lends no man its aid.
> The children their unsmiling kingdoms keep,
> And I walk with them, and I am afraid.

There is in fact a great deal more art in Causley's work than may
appear at first sight. In immediate impact, entertaining speakability,
comic attack and even in social comment, he is much superior to the
'pop' poets who use some of the same themes and who may seem to
have some of the same appeal. 'Reservoir Street', 'Demolition
Order', 'Devonport', and 'Hospital' have a gritty basis of realism,
and 'The Visit' a persistence of observation and a finely controlled
contempt, that show ambitious areas into which Causley is
penetrating. A Causley poem is instantly recognizable and always
fresh.

7

'The Movement' and after: Philip Larkin, Kingsley Amis, Robert Conquest, Elizabeth Jennings, D.J. Enright, John Wain, Donald Davie, Thom Gunn

'The Movement' – the bareness of the title has sometimes been interpreted as arrogance, sometimes as mere blankness – is still occasionally a topic of literary polemics. Did it exist? If it did, who belonged to it? And did it achieve anything, or was it (as Ian Hamilton has put it) something with 'its distinctive niche in the history of publicity – it was a take-over bid and it brilliantly succeeded'?

An essay which takes as its starting point the early 1960s is not the place to plot the early moves in this campaign (if one accepts Hamilton's notion that there was a campaign), nor its supposed documents of the 1950s – *New Lines,* the poetry magazine *Listen,* the review columns of the *Spectator* and so on. When Robert Conquest edited *New Lines 2* in 1963, he remarked in his Introduction that Donald Davie had suggested a suitable title for the section containing poems by the original figures (Philip Larkin, Kingsley Amis, D.J. Enright, Thom Gunn, Elizabeth Jennings, John Wain, and Conquest and Davie themselves), might be 'Divergent Lines'; and one takes the point. If anything yoked the originals together in 1956, it was not apparent by 1963. And if *New Lines 2* could include Ted Hughes (as it did), wasn't it in fact embracing the 'dynamic romanticism' that critics of the Old Movement had called for? Blake Morrison's magisterial critical book *The Movement* (1980) examines all this in detail, as a slice of history.

If one is talking about merit rather than tactics, poets and poems rather than literary history, one thing seems indisputable; to quote Ian Hamilton again,

> at one level, it could be said that Philip Larkin's poems
> provide a precise model for what the Movement was

Philip Larkin
(Photograph Fay Godwin)

supposed to be seeking. But having noted his lucidity, his debunkery, his technical accomplishment and other such 'typical' attributes, one would still be left with the different and deeper task of describing the quality of his peculiar genius . . . †

Larkin's achievement has been recognized even by critics who are suspicious of his supposed 'attitudes' and who are contemptuous of the poets who were enlisted with him into the Movement. This was clear in the years following the publication of *The Less Deceived* (1955) and *New Lines,* and when *The Whitsun Weddings* eventually followed in 1964 it was confirmed.

With the publication of *High Windows* (1974), and in the years since, there has been a consolidation of the general – both critical and popular – view that Philip Larkin is the finest living poet writing in English. It is a view that rests on a small body of work – fewer than a hundred poems are included in the three mature books – and Larkin has added less than a single handful since *High Windows*. But the book assembled for his sixtieth birthday (*Larkin at Sixty,* 1982), together with the great majority of the book's reviews, showed a degree of affection, touched with amusement and anecdotery, which must be unique among readers of twentieth-century English poetry.

Innocence, the pathos and grim humour of experience, the poignancy of the past (whether one's own remembered past or the imagined past of another century), the change and renewal of nature, the dread of the future, death and all that leads up to it and away from it: such listing of the subject-matter of Larkin's poems quickly runs itself into flat abstractions, totally lacking the precise circumstantial figurativeness and sensitive cadences of the poems themselves. Larkin has said that a good poem is both 'sensitive' and 'efficient' – two more abstractions, but ones that are given flesh when one reads such poems as 'The Building', 'The Old Fools', 'Sad Steps', 'The Explosion', or – slightly earlier – 'The Whitsun Weddings' and 'An Arundel Tomb'. 'The Building' opens with a typically dense and carefully selected proliferation of impressionist detail, so organized that it is only gradually one realizes that the place being described is a hospital: as in 'Church Going' and 'The Whitsun Weddings', the detail is an embodiment of the poem, not the casual decoration its

† From 'The Making of the Movement' in *A Poetry Chronicle,* 1973.

40

colloquial ease at first suggests:

> on the way
> Someone's wheeled past, in washed-to-rags ward clothes:
> They see him, too. They're quiet. To realise
> This new thing held in common makes them quiet,
> For past these doors are rooms, and rooms past those,
> And more rooms yet, each one further off
> And harder to return from . . .

And in the end, relentlessly poised like the train in 'The Whitsun Weddings', the realization towards which the whole delicate structure has been aimed is achieved:

> All know they are going to die.
> Not yet, perhaps not here, but in the end,
> And somewhere like this. That is what it means,
> This clean-sliced cliff; a struggle to transcend
> The thought of dying, for unless its powers
> Outbuild cathedrals nothing contravenes
> The coming dark, though crowds each evening try
>
> With wasteful, weak, propitiatory flowers.

The stanzaic and rhymed structure of 'The Building', typically, is so unobtrusive, draws so little superficial attention to itself, that only a closer look reveals how tightly organized it is. Each seven-line stanza is completely consistent in its rhyme scheme, but the first line of each stanza picks up the rhyme in the fifth line of the stanza preceding it, so that the whole poem can be seen to be made up of interlinked quatrains (ABCB:DCAD), the 'trailing' rhyme picking up the serpentine movement and running it on. To those who may think such considerations trivial, mere fingering of an old-fashioned instrument, there are many possible answers: one is that it works.
Sometimes Larkin deals with his habitual themes of diminution,

decay, death, in an extreme and even savage way, as he does in 'Sunny Prestatyn', in which the blandishments of the girl on the poster have been desecrated and disproved. The opening of 'The Old Fools' – looking at geriatric patients in what is, in ordinary euphemistic terms, called 'an old people's home' – has something of the same feeling:

> What do they think has happened, the old fools,
> To make them like this? Do they somehow suppose
> It's more grown-up when your mouth hangs open and drools,
> And you keep on pissing yourself and can't remember
> Who called this morning?

But such savagery always turns back on itself in Larkin, and is often seen with fear and horror. The triumph is that of art. Clive James has written of him that he is 'the poet of the void. The one affirmation his work offers is the possibility that when we have lost everything the problem of beauty will still remain.'

Even Larkin's least elevated, most casually light poems have a refined, unobtrusive, but technically formidable skill, able to accommodate colloquial language and colloquial rhythms: 'Posterity', for example, which casts a cold eye on 'Jake Balokowsky, my biographer', and 'Vers de Société', which balances boring sociability against the pleasures and desolations of solitude. Both serious and light have the distinctive, sad, subtle and palpable flavour of an individual with the loyalties, exasperations, prejudices, illuminations and speaking voice of a distinctly irreducible character. Part of Larkin's breadth of appeal comes from the many kinds of poem this character can appear in: variety within unity. From the evocation of nineteenth-century emigrants (in 'How Distant') or colliers (in 'The Explosion') to the lyrical naturalism of 'The Trees' and 'Cut Grass', the breadth of sympathies is wide, the voice unmistakable, however wan the tone:

> The trees are coming into leaf
> Like something almost being said;
> The recent buds relax and spread,

Their greenness is a kind of grief.

Is it that they are born again
And we grow old? No, they die too.
Their yearly trick of looking new
Is written down in rings of grain.

Yet still the unresting castles thresh
In fullgrown thickness every May.
Last year is dead, they seem to say,
Begin afresh, afresh, afresh.

('The Trees')★

Individual though Larkin is, he often reflects common experiences
and common concerns. He has no easy answers, but he does not
wallow in fashionable *angst* either. As far as 'public' concerns go, he
has touched on such things in some poems (such as 'Going, Going'
and 'Homage to a Government'), showing attitudes that are
conservative and even 'reactionary' – in this, though in little else,
reminding one of Yeats and Eliot. But unlike any other important
modern British poet, Larkin has constructed no system into which
his poems can snugly fit: like Parolles in Shakespeare's *All's Well,* he
seems to say 'simply the thing I am shall make me live'.

The coarse, genial, unillusioned talent of Kingsley Amis is very
like one facet of Larkin's – that side of Larkin which delivers itself of
such dicta as 'Get stewed. Books are a load of crap.' Amis manages
this very well, in his poems as in his prose fiction. The worm's-eye-
view commemorated in his sequence 'The Evans Country'
entertainingly exposes hypocrisies and furtive sexual goings-on of
all sorts, grinning, unjudging, triumphant. The hypocrisies are
pretensions about art as well as about morality:

Hearing how tourists, dazed with reverence,
Look through sunglasses at the Parthenon,
I thought of that cold night outside the Gents
When Dai touched Gwyneth up with his gloves on.

('Aldport (Mystery Tour)'★

In this narrow area of 'come off it', Amis's touch is as sure as Dai's: when he tries affirmation, as in such love poems as 'Oligodora', 'Green Heart', 'Waking Beauty' and 'A Point of Logic', he becomes a pasticheur of Graves. Apart from this, the danger with Amis is that he too easily turns into a self-caricaturist, emphasizing too cheaply a small number of routine assumptions, whether his target is Jesus Christ (in 'New Approach Needed') or himself (in his poem on his fiftieth birthday).

Among the poets corralled into the Movement, Amis – for all his entertainment value – is one of those who, like Robert Conquest and Elizabeth Jennings, seems almost to have stood still. Conquest's best poems have always been hard-edged bits of experience, not the frigid deliberations about art, verse, love and sex which have made up most of his efforts: in *Arias from a Love Opera,* 'Then' and 'Existences: Zurich' are good examples of his descriptive intensity, 'Measure of All Things' of his teasing eroticism. Elizabeth Jennings is more impressive. Her *Collected Poems,* published in 1967, gathered work over a period of fifteen years and showed a steady and persistent contemplative gift, rational but open to mystery, tender but unsentimental, expressed in forms and words that were almost always pure, clear, gravely lyrical and committed to a sense of hard-won order out of chaos. In 'One Flesh', she looks at her parents:

> Strangely apart, yet strangely close together,
> Silence between them like a thread to hold
> And not wind in. And time itself's a feather
> Touching them gently. Do they know they're old,
> These two who are my father and my mother
> Whose fire, from which I came, has now grown cold?

The clarity and cool formality were imposed on personal, confessional material, fixing and assuaging turbulence and disorder by speaking so calmly and in such level tones, as in the beginning of her poem 'Patients', one of a 'Sequence in Hospital':

Violence does not terrify.
Storms here would be a relief,
Lightning be a companion to grief.
It is the helplessness, the way they lie

Beyond hope, fear, love,
That makes me afraid. I would like to shout,
Crash my voice into the silence, flout
The passive suffering here . . .

Elizabeth Jennings has published half a dozen books since the *Collected Poems,* but none has quite had the impact of her best earlier work. There has been a thinning away into a simplicity that sometimes looks like banality; but now and then, in *Growing-Points* (1975) and *Moments of Grace* (1979) particularly, there are nakedly direct poems which remind one of her former strengths and have something of the intensity of Emily Dickinson:

I feel I could be turned to ice
If this goes on, if this goes on.
I feel I could be buried twice
And still the death not yet be done.

I feel I could be turned to fire
If there can be no end to this.
I know within me such desire
No kiss could satisfy, no kiss.

I feel I could be turned to stone,
A solid block not carved at all,
Because I feel so much alone.
I could be grave-stone or a wall.

But better to be turned to earth
Where other things at least can grow.
I could be then a part of birth,
Passive, not knowing how to know.   ('I Feel')★

D.J. Enright showed in his *Collected Poems* (1981) that he was not only the humane, amusing, commonsensical, wanly indignant annotator of the social brutalities and masqueradings of a world that stretches, if not from China to Peru, then from Thailand to the English Midlands, but also a clever constructer of sequences: *The Terrible Shears* looked at his own upbringing as the son of an Irish immigrant, while *Paradise Illustrated* and *A Faust Book* were witty, downbeat variations on themes by Milton and Goethe:

> 'Why didn't we think of clothes before?'
> Asked Adam,
> Removing Eve's.
>
> 'Why did we ever think of clothes?'
> Asked Eve,
> Laundering Adam's.
>
> (xxii from *Paradise Illustrated*)★

The three Movement poets who have gone furthest in changing what had been their early manners are John Wain, Donald Davie and Thom Gunn. Each has followed a different progression – Wain from metronomic Empsonian measures to free-ranging and sometimes garrulous inclusiveness, Davie from polished neo-Augustanisms to more oblique and glancing moments of perception, and Gunn (most interestingly) from what he has called his early 'clenched' verse through experiments with syllabics reminiscent of some contemporary Americans to the formal but liberated insights of *Moly,* some of which was apparently written under the influence of hallucinogenic drugs.

Wain's more recent books, such as *Wildtrack* (1965), *Letters to Five Artists* (1969) and *Feng* (1975), are long, loosely organized sequences. The blurb to the second book says that it indicates, 'once again, Mr Wain's faith in poetry as a vehicle for major statements'. The arrogant obtuseness of this is a fair comment on what is wrong with much of *Wildtrack* and *Letters* – an irritably impatient self-importance which lunges towards 'major statements' without earning the right to make them. In *Wildtrack,* the Russian

Revolution, the growth of mass production in the advent of the Ford car, Dr Johnson, Dean Swift, Rousseau, an 'Oration to all the beggars in the world', the creation of Adam and sundry dreams are all roughly hurled into the same mixture, in a conflicting variety of forms as arbitrary as they are various. The leaps and plunges mime a desperate uncertainty rather than intrepid exploration, so that the rapt sensuality of the Baudelairean sonnet 'to Jeanne Duval' is facetiously demolished with 'The day God slipped Adam a Mickey Finn!' The form of *Letters* draws much less attention to itself, being basically iambic pentameter, but here the trouble lies in diffuseness and a dogged rhetoric in which bits of fine and eloquent poetry are submerged. One can admire the height of Wain's ambition without being convinced that he has got anywhere near achieving it. His most impressive poems are still some of those included in *Weep Before God* (1961): 'Au Jardin des Plantes', 'Anecdote of 2 a.m.', and – certainly ambitious, but with an authoritative unifying strength – 'A Song about Major Eatherly'.

Donald Davie's free adaptation of Mickiewicz's *Pan Tadeusz*, called *The Forests of Lithuania*, showed as early as 1959 that this poet was not content to remain what he himself called 'a pasticheur of late Augustan styles'. Since then he has published several more books of verse and two *Collected Poems*. *Events and Wisdoms* (1964) showed a metaphorical richness which was not much in evidence before, a visual relish and a sensuous awareness of the world – the river delta in 'Low Lands', for example:

> Like a snake it is, its serpentine iridescence
> Of slow light spilt and wheeling over calm
> Inundations, and a snake's still menace
> Hooding with bruised sky belfry and lonely farm

This is the landscape, too, of many of his *Essex Poems* (1969), but here the style has been stripped down to something less mellifluous, more angular, intent perhaps on *not* making final, tidy statements but on leaving the poems open:

It is not life being short,
Death certain, that is making
Those faintly coffee-coloured
Gridiron marks on the snow
Or that row of trees heart-breaking.

What stirs us when a curtain
Of ice-hail dashes the window?
It is the wasteness of space
That a man drives wagons into
Or plants his windbreak in.

Spaces stop time from hurting.
Over verst on verst of Russia
Are lime-tree avenues.

('A Winter Landscape Near Ely')★

In other poems Davie uses a tentative, slightly stumbling, rather Pasternak-like quatrain form for his observations, nervously energetic, full of rapid leaps of thought and angular compressions, with comment that rapidly fills in persons, places, history and social ironies with a few strokes. He has an unsettled, sharply intelligent talent, and the two volumes of *Collected Poems* show his shifts and turns well.

Thom Gunn's third book, *My Sad Captains* (1961), contained a few poems – 'The Feel of Hands', 'Considering the Snail', 'Flying Above California', and others – which seemed to indicate a turning-point. They were tentative, unselfassertive, much more broken in their rhythms than the aggressively masculine (yet oddly vulnerable) poems that had been his trademark in *Fighting Terms* and *The Sense of Movement*. Gunn has always been a poet who makes an active use of *pose,* in matter as in manner – for example, the notorious lines:

I think of all the toughs through history
And thank heaven they lived, continually.

('Lines for a Book')

But in *My Sad Captains* the pose was different, and the voice not a strong-lined one adapted from Donne and the later Yeats but one apparently learned from such American poets as William Carlos Williams and Marianne Moore. (Gunn has been resident in the US for many years.) What Martin Dodsworth has described as 'a seeping from line to line, which we must follow in a careful, groping movement of the mind' reached its most extreme point in *Touch* (1967). Here the title-poem is tender, even sentimental, in its casual perceptions about a man nestling into bed with his lover in the dark:

> Meanwhile and slowly
> I feel a is it
> my own warmth surfacing or
> the ferment of your whole
> body that in darkness beneath
> the cover is stealing
> bit by bit to break
> down that chill.

The trouble here, as in other poems in the book, is that the perceptions too quickly seem dreamy and insubstantial, loaded down with too much undifferentiated detail, the words running on amiably but without pressure – 'a warm clutter of detail', to take a phrase from one of Gunn's poems.

One could not make such objections to 'Misanthropos', the long sequence following the cycle of activities of the last surviving man after an atomic war: this poem from *Touch* seemed to be a bridgehead, or an amalgam from which Gunn was to choose a definitively achieved style, when *Moly* was published in 1971. *Moly* contained the best poems he had written for a long time: they have the fine-drawn tension, the firm iambic tread, of his early poems, but blazing through them is an exalted sense of illumination, an irradiated sensuousness that is quite new – as in 'The Fair in the Woods':

Landscape of acid:
                where on fern and mound
The lights fragmented by the roofing bough
Throbbed outward, joining over broken ground
To one long dazzling burst; as even now
Horn closes over horn into one sound.

Gunn's most recent books, *Jack Straw's Castle* (1976) and *The Passages of Joy* (1982), are both more relaxed and more mixed, and they show that he has become a fluid and even an uncertain writer, open to a variety of styles which can co-exist. For example, *Jack Straw's Castle,* drawing as it does on a number of more directly personal sources than has been usual in Gunn, contains the loose, Gary Snyder-like 'Autobiography' and the formal, gently lyrical 'Last Days at Teddington':

The sniff of the real, that's
what I'd want to get
        how it felt
to sit on Parliament
Hill on a May evening
studying for exams   skinny
seventeen   dissatisfied
        yet sniffing such
a potent air, smell of
grass in heat from
the day's sun

            ('Autobiography')

So coming back from drinking late
We picked our way below the wall
But in the higher grass, dewed wet,
Stumbled on tricycle and ball.

When everything was moved away,
The house returned to board and shelf,
And smelt of hot dust through the day,
The garden fell back on itself.

('Last Days at Teddington')

8

Vernon Scannell, Dannie Abse, Patricia Beer, Laurence Lerner, John Fuller, Clive James

Edward Lucie-Smith has written that 'The aftermath of the Movement began almost as soon as the Movement itself', an observation that shows the remarkable telescoping that literary journalists are apt to impose. It is true that there are a number of congenial poets who could easily have been drafted into *New Lines* without strain, and sadly some of them even found themselves briefly conscripted into an anthology which purported to represent the opposition – so confused has been what Alvarez has called the 'gang-warfare which, at a distance, can be dignified as disagreements between schools of verse'. Both Vernon Scannell and Dannie Abse were represented in this anthology (*Mavericks*, 1957 – Abse indeed was the book's co-editor); but they have by now detached themselves from such dubious literary history and can be seen as good poets in their own right.

Scannell's best work dates from the early 1960s, and his well-chosen *New and Collected Poems 1950– 1980* demonstrates it: colloquial, easy in its manner, realistically urban and anecdotal, poised above a romantic pessimism that senses irony almost everywhere but would, one feels, like to make a stronger and more positive gesture. They are attractive poems rooted in felt experience: 'Dead Dog', 'The Telephone Number', 'Hide and Seek', 'I'm Covered Now' and 'Walking Wounded' keep the focus clearly fixed on that experience. When he goes wrong it is almost always because of careless or contrived language. The same can be said of Abse, a poet whose strategy is similar but who is more given to whimsy: this can be lightly charming, as in 'Not Adlestrop', but he is best when he still sticks to quiddities but goes deeper into them, as he does in 'Olfactory Pursuits':

A man sniffs the back of his own hand,
moistens it with his mouth, to sniff again,
to think a blank; writes, 'The odour of stones'.

Both Scannell and Abse are poets who use ordinary, mundane concerns with skill.

Laurence Lerner, Patricia Beer and (from a rather later generation) John Fuller write alert, intelligent poems that are more often concerned not so much with catching moments of experience but with constructing artefacts. This is least true of Patricia Beer, who often writes with a mixture of plain statement and a rather droll sense of irony; but she does not rest comfortably in irony, as do many lesser poets with her kind of talent, but worries away at something deeper, the sources of her need to achieve an elegant detachment, as in the closing lines of 'Self-Help':

> And through
> The white comfortable mist a wind blows holes,
> Lays bare the quagmire reaching for us all,
> Whispers how soon we could be shouting 'Help.'

Laurence Lerner is more inventive, and his most noticed recent work has been two sequences which pretend to have been written by a computer: *A.R.T.H.U.R.* (1974) and *A.R.T.H.U.R. & M.A.R.T.H.A.* (1980). Both are very funny and ingenious, but some of his best poems take constructed or reconstructed figures and give them life, as monologues or spoken addresses, as in 'The Merman', 'Saskia', 'Years Later', 'The Experiment', and 'The Three German Ladies of Rimini'. Other Lerner poems are exercises in style which go beyond technical trickery, though that is where they start:

> Wogs rats pigs dogs
> Don't stay here, they said.
> Move away; else stay dead.
> Sail home. Move over.
> Don't stay ever.   ('Poem in Four-letter Words')

John Fuller's first book, *Fairground Music,* was chiefly a young man's display of elegant skill and wit – not bad wares for a very young poet to show. His many succeeding books have continued to show them, but with a much more impressive inventiveness and an extended scale. He is riddling, teasing, a virtuoso of forms, whether in the five *Epistles to Several Persons* (1973), his comic verse tale *The Illusionists* (1980), which is written in the stanza-form of Pushkin's *Eugene Onegin,* or in the games, songs, monologues, squibs, rococo fantasies and extravagant machinery that make up *Lies and Secrets* (1979). But this last book also shows that the dazzling performer is capable of real and piercing feeling: Fuller showed it earlier, in poems of the disturbances of a haunted suburbia ('Alive and Dead', 'Green Fingers', 'Goodbye to the Garden'), and here it is represented by two poems concerned with a dead friend, 'In the Corridor' and 'In the Hotel'★:

Where was it, then, that I saw my dead friend?
The hotel with breakfast beneath a curving stair?
The hotel under the eaves and the spouting gutters?
The hotel of darkness? The hotel of black marble?
The hotel of dead water with its dripping
And lead wounds and stumps of extempore plumbing?

All our days flourished in their bound ledger!
The accounts are kept open for the unforeseen
Yet absolutely necessary expenditure.
Sleepless we think, we are driving in our sleep
To arrive in the end at the commercial hotel
With its frail balcony above the empty streets.

Sleepless, are yet asleep and not asleep,
The room is airless, change piled on the washstand,
The pipes sighing all night with water or air
In whichever hotel it was that I saw my friend,
Where we ourselves must wake on the final day
In the last and least remembered hotel of all.

Clive James in the 1970s and 1980s has made a wide popular reputation for himself both as a very funny columnist (he was for some years television critic of the *Observer*) and as an equally funny and adept verse satirist. His best verse is contained in the first of his 'mock epics', *Peregrine Prykke's Pilgrimage Through the London Literary World,* (1976), a genially ribald narrative in couplets which peppers many lightly-disguised targets among writers, editors and publishers; and also in some of the seven verse letters which make up *Fan-Mail* (1977). One of these is to the playwright Tom Stoppard, and makes plain James's contempt for much contemporary theatre – though not, of course, Stoppard's:

> If dramas do not hammer Themes
> Like pub bores telling you their dreams
>   The dense don't twig.
> They want the things they know already
> Reiterated loud and steady –
>   Drilled through the wig.

('To Tom Stoppard: A Letter from London')

9

Ted Hughes and Sylvia Plath

Under the orthodox system of appraisal which can see only one
dominant poet at a time (MacSpaunday was an exception), the
retrospective list seems to run: Eliot, Dylan Thomas, Larkin, Ted
Hughes – a neat apportioning of one poet per decade. The orthodoxy
is irrelevant, because poetry does not operate under the same rules as
the popular record industry, whereby last week's fashions must be
rapidly discarded to make way for the new. But there can be no
doubt that within the decade of the 1960s Ted Hughes was accepted
as a classic of our time, his books becoming set texts in schools, and
very large claims have been made for him: A. Alvarez has called him
'a poet of the first importance'.

The basis for this was the work in *The Hawk in the Rain* (1957)
and *Lupercal* (1960) – work which concentrated on physical vividness
of a mimetic sort, in a turbulent world of predatory animals,
primitive violence and moments of extreme human endurance – a
bloody world ruled by impulse and instinct, with 'No indolent
procrastinations and no yawning stares/No sighs or
head-scratchings'. But for all their ferocity, the poems in these books
are highly organized and concentrated: in the best of them the animal
energy is ruthlessly contained (in 'Hawk Roosting' or 'View of a
Pig', for example), the spareness of utterance allowing greater clarity
and coherence.

After that, between 1960 and 1967, Hughes published only
some pamphlet collections and children's verse. *Wodwo* (1967)
contains some short stories and an unsatisfactory verse-play, 'The
Wound', together with some poems in the manner of his best
('Thistles', 'Fern' and, less neatly but with considerable bravura
effects, 'Skylarks'), and others which seemed to come from a
fascination with primitive poetry, runic spells and mystic
incantations, a shamanistic hotch-potch:

> And right through the smile
> That is the judge's fury
> That is the wailing child

Ted Hughes
(Photograph Mark Gerson)

That is the ribboned gift
That is the starved adder
That is the kiss in the dream
That is the nightmare pillow
That is the seal of resemblances
That is illusion
That is illusion

The rider of iron, on the horse shod with vaginas of iron,
Gallops over the womb that makes no claim, that is of stone.

('Gog')

To my mind, *Crow* (1970) is an extension of this. This sequence, which was described when it was first published as 'the passages of verse from about the first two-thirds of what was to have been an epic folk-tale', was an immediate cause of controversy. To some it was a major poem, a work of genius; the central symbol was 'a new hero' – though that may have been ironically meant. Elsewhere there were some small protesting noises about Hughes's 'apparently deliberate resort to primitive hamfisted adjectives and trudging monosyllabic phrases', and his 'mechanical, drugging repetition'. Whatever the consensus, *Crow* has certainly entered the poetry-reading consciousness, and its manner or manners have been widely imitated and even parodied – a firm indication that a work has 'arrived'.

Crow basically has two characters – Crow himself and God. Crow is resilient, resourceful, evasive, built to survive every kind of disaster: he is a protean figure, but these are his irreducible characteristics. God is sometimes his partner, sometimes his adversary or rival, often a passive presence who goes on sleeping while Crow gets up to his gruesome tricks:

Crow laughed.
He bit the Worm, God's only son,
Into two writhing halves.

He stuffed into man the tail half
With the wounded end hanging out.

He stuffed the head half headfirst into woman
And it crept in deeper and up
To peer out through her eyes
Calling its tail-half to join up quickly, quickly
Because O it was painful.

('A Childish Prank')

The manner of *Crow* is almost all like this – a series of unmodified
narrative accounts of brutally comic (or just brutally brutal) events,
sometimes varied with catalogues of incantations (very like the
passage from *Wodwo* quoted above) or lists of questions
('Who . . . ?', 'Where . . . ?'), all of which are common devices in
oral poetry from the pre-literate world – a genre one knows Hughes
admires, and indeed 'Two Eskimo Songs' form part of the *Crow*
sequence.

This kind of procedure – which some critics, trying to find some
phenomenon nearer twentieth-century Britain to which to relate
Crow, have likened to the technique of the horror-comic, with its
crude devices of BAM! SPLAT! ZOWY! – is a compendious one.
Anything, so long as it lacks verbal or rhythmical subtlety and is
painted in primary colours, can fit into it. But what is *Crow* about,
beyond its manner? Some have answered 'Survival' – that of the
merest subsistence, against mercilessly inimical forces. More nearly,
it seems to me, it poses in aggressive terms an old-fashioned
theology or demonology – a Manichean duality which Augustine
would have recognized; did, in fact, recognize, and rejected because
it was simple-minded in its refusal to see the world in other than
dogmatically pessimistic and exclusive terms – arbitrary,
unarguable, assuming an esoteric revelation that by-passes reason
and substitutes assertion for truth:

Crow realized there were two Gods –

One of them much bigger than the other
Loving his enemies
And having all the weapons.

('Crow's Theology')

59

The ambiguities in this are all in the interpretation, never in the assertion: in this, Hughes in a sense puts himself beyond criticism. But judged solely as technical constructs, the *Crow* poems can properly be called monotonous, relying as they do on endless repetitions of a few rhetorical devices and a few key words (black, blood, smashed, stabbed, screamed). As with the paintings of Francis Bacon, a totality of horror is narrowly and intensely insisted, and in the end pays low dividends, because the trick, once noticed, is a diminishing one. Language is no longer a medium but a message, and the world is no longer something to be particularized (as it was in *The Hawk in the Rain* and *Lupercal*) but is retreated from. It is an abnegation not only from poetry but from wisdom.

Since *Crow*, Hughes has been more prolific than ever. *Cave Birds* (sub-titled resonantly but unilluminatingly as 'An Alchemical Cave Drama') is a sequence of twenty-nine poems written to accompany drawings by Leonard Baskin (whose menacing pictures of crows originally inspired *Crow*) of anthropomorphic imaginary birds, and can be seen as an extension of *Crow's* emblematic symbolism. *Season Songs* was bracketed off by Hughes's publishers as 'for children', but this modestly diminishing description does not disguise the poems' concentration, vividness and attack, or their more relaxed extension of the keen-eyed poet of *Lupercal* sixteen years earlier: 'The Stag', a cumulatively dramatic and moving picture of a stag hunt, and 'Swifts' are among his very best poems. *Gaudete* is held by a few devoted Hughes disciples to be the peak of his achievement; but to many others this long treatment of an Anglican clergyman possessed by 'powers of the other world' is a ludicrous travesty, unrelieved by the 'Epilogue' of verses at the end supposedly written by the Reverend Lumb. *Remains of Elmet* was another work that took its support from a visual source, this time photographs by Fay Godwin of parts of the Pennine moorland of Yorkshire where Hughes spent much of his childhood. Some of its component poems come to grips splendidly with the bleak topography and history of this landscape, a mixture of natural beauty and derelict industrialism:

> Streets bent to the task
> Of holding it all up
> Bracing themselves, taking the strain
> Till their vertebrae slipped.

> ('When Men got to the Summit')

Moortown is a sort of hold-all, with four books (or sequences) in one set of covers. The first, 'Moortown' itself, includes some of Hughes's finest poems, its material relating to that of *Season Songs*. In a note in the volume, it was typically played down by Hughes as being 'made up of passages taken from a verse farming diary that I kept for a while'. The setting is rural Devon, where Hughes has lived for many years. The word 'diary' is perhaps meant to allow for informality, even casualness, but many of the poems themselves have a degree of intensity, sanity and rapt grace that he has never equalled, as in 'February 17th', a powerfully resolute and exact account of delivering a lamb which had to be killed to save the mother:

> Then like
> Pulling myself to the ceiling with one finger
> Hooked in a loop, timing my effort
> To her birth push groans, I pulled against
> The corpse that would not come. Till it came.
> And after it the long, sudden, yolk-yellow
> Parcel of life
> In a smoking slither of oils and soups and syrups –
> And the body lay born, beside the hacked-off head.
>
> ('February 17th')

The other three sections in *Moortown* are 'Prometheus on his Crag', 'Adam and the Sacred Nine', and 'Earth-numb'. All are further cryptic texts drawing on myths and using the same bare rhetorical devices as the *Crow* poems, with the same portentous grimness but without even their occasional flashes of primitive humour. Hughes has a copious and impressive talent – there is no doubt about that; but it is a talent which seems to change direction, soar, lose height, lose itself, recover, and then inexplicably repeat its own worst faults, again and again. His *Selected Poems 1957–1981* (1982) shows this, and also serves to show much arbitrariness in Hughes's own selection from what were originally presented as indissoluble sequences. Hughes continues to be a major force in English poetry, widely read, but readers have not quite brought to his work the affection they bring to his rather older contemporary, Larkin, or his rather

younger one, Seamus Heaney; and among his peers, his fellow
poets, he is probably rated below Geoffrey Hill (see pp. 82–88.)

Hughes's work is inextricably linked with that of his wife,
Sylvia Plath, who committed suicide early in 1963. In a way,
Hughes's poems are the *animus* to her *anima* – the male principle
backing onto the female principle on the same coin: compare, for
example, his 'Thistles' with her 'Mushrooms'. Sylvia Plath died
towards the beginning of the period with which this essay deals, but
her work appeared in posthumous books throughout the next
decade and has gained a considerable following, even a cult of
impassioned believers and commentators. She is still very much a
live force in English poetry, into which has been woven an extremist
legend of a doomed artist bent on self-destruction. The hysteria,
memorializing aggrandisement, interpretative ludicrousness and
plain bad judgement of what has been called 'the Plath industry' are
unpleasantly reminiscent of the ballyhoo that followed the death of
Dylan Thomas ten years earlier. It seems not so much that art needs
its victims but that the susceptible reading public does.

Sylvia Plath's posthumously published *Ariel* (1965) is the crucial
collection, now fully augmented and placed in its context in the
Collected Poems (1981). The poems that have had most attention have
naturally enough been those in *Ariel,* because there has been more
time to assimilate them; but because much of that book was written
during the downward spin which brought her to her suicide, it is
unbalanced to think of her as most importantly the poet of such
death-infatuated pieces as 'Daddy' and 'Lady Lazarus' – these were
the final spurts of lava from the volcano. The volcano image may
seem as hysterical as the responses I have just been chiding, but it is
meant to convey the feeling in Plath's work of dormant pressure:
most of her poems are the wisps of smoke above the cone, indicating
but not embodying the violence below. A large number of them are
vividly and warmly celebratory, intent on what Barbara Hardy has
called 'imaginative enlargement' – of candles, for example:

> I watch their spilt tears cloud and dull to pearls.
> How shall I tell anything at all
> To this infant still in a birth-drowse?
> Tonight, like a shawl, the mild light enfolds her,
> The shadows stoop over like guests at a christening.

> ('Candles')

62

Or of an old man convalescing (in 'Among the Narcissi'):

> There is a dignity to this; there is a formality –
> The flowers vivid as bandages, and the man mending.
> They bow and stand: they suffer such attacks!
>
> And the octogenarian loves the little flocks.
> He is quite blue; the terrible wind tries his breathing.
> The narcissi look up like children, quickly and whitely.

In these poems, and in many others in *Crossing the Water* and *Winter Trees* as well as *Ariel,* she is very far from being that patron saint of the nervous breakdown which her imitators would have her be. The felt life, the exuberant observation, the freshness and efficiency of her sensuous apprehension of the world flash out and blossom again and again. This is not to diminish the serious intensity of her obsessively disturbed poems but to put them in their proper perspective as statements that are no more 'final' (except in a chronological sense) than the rest of her prolific output. She was a remarkably poised and controlled poet, and we do her work a disservice if we put our best effort into lauding the poems written when that poise began to falter and her creative will lost control.

In the wake of Ted Hughes and Sylvia Plath there is a whole 'Tribe of Ted' – poets who have adopted subjects, mannerisms, even vocabulary. Some of them, such as Seamus Heaney, are freer of direct influences than others, and have staked out their own specialities and excellences. Some have added a dash of winsomeness, or water, and seem like diluted versions of the originals. A few – such as Jon Silkin and Peter Redgrove – began with their own strong personalities and have assimilated only what suited them. Harold Massingham, Ted Walker, David Wevill and Glyn Hughes can all be seen to fit into these categories.

The shared subject-matter is usually drawn from anthropomorphized Nature – in other words, the earlier poems of Ted Hughes have been a more potent influence here than the later. Reading some English poetry these days, a foreigner might be forgiven for supposing that the Industrial Revolution had never taken place, that most of us don't live in conurbations, and that we spend our time following the plough or tickling trout. It is true that in modern times there have been a few – a very few – good poets whose work has been pure 'Nature Poetry': Andrew Young (who died in 1971, and who had written no poems for many years before that) is a name which immediately comes to mind. But from Wordsworth to Edward Thomas and beyond, the poetry of Nature and the poetry of the human have intersected. They still do, of course, and to most modern Englishmen the appeal of stoats, baders, pike, eagles and adders, together with any knowledge of crop husbandry, the mating habits of bulls or even what the clouds foretell, must be primarily vicarious or nostalgic, or symbolic.

It is as symbols that these creatures and properties proliferate in the work of the poets I have named:

There are other ways than this:
there are ways only he knows.
In a rickyard where rats are
he could circle, coil his neck,
and with wings at the trail, thrash straw
and spike what he cared to spike.

('Heron': Ted Walker)

What had become of the young shark?
It was time for the ocean to move on.
Somehow, sheathed in the warm current
He'd lost his youthful bite, and fell
Shuddering among the feelers of kelp
And dragging weeds. His belly touched sand,
The shark ran aground on his shadow.

('The Birth of Shark': David Wevill)

Spawning and nibbling, the ram is the Big Dick.
Those fish that nibble a man to the bone
whilst he swims, have nothing on him . . .

('Sheep': Glyn Hughes)

Brains blacker than blackberries, bellow and eyes
Blackening in defence of apples: he stands
A watch-bull squarely on four black feet;
Enough to make handsome any paradise.

('Black Bull Guarding Apples': Harold Massingham)

The door, unbolted, whacked back against the wall.
The illegal sire fumbled from his stall

Unhurried, as an old steam engine shunting.
He circled, snored and nosed. No hectic panting,

Just the unfussy ease of a good tradesman;
Then an awkward, unexpected jump, and

His knobbled forelegs straddling her flank,
He slammed life home, impassive as a tank,

('The Outlaw': Seamus Heaney)

Just as electric pylons seemed to some poets of the 1930s 'the quick perspective of the future' (Spender's phrase), so these wild creatures and rural emblems seem links with a vanishing past. The common way of looking, the common tone, of the mini-anthology I have compiled above is remarkable. All these poets have a strong line in descriptive mimetics, comparable with Ted Hughes's 'The Jaguar' and 'The Bull Moses'; but in a curious way it seems a form of escapism, pre-ecological stuff at a time when we are quickly approaching a state when (as Larkin has put it)

                    all that remains
    For us will be concrete and tyres.

10

'The Group' and after:
Peter Porter, George MacBeth,
Peter Redgrove, Alan Brownjohn,
Edwin Brock, Fleur Adcock,
Jenny Joseph

One 'community of letters' that as early as the mid-1950s was taking
notice of Ted Hughes, even before the publication of *The Hawk in the
Rain,* was the so-called 'Group' – a loosely-organized assemblage of
poets who (first in Cambridge under the chairmanship of Philip
Hobsbaum, then – and more importantly – at Edward Lucie-Smith's
house in London) met once a week to discuss one another's poems in
an atmosphere of watchful sobriety, rigorously unsparing criticism,
and to a less certain extent mutual esteem and emulation. The Group
has now dispersed, but several of its members still show some of the
characteristics (or bear the scars) of that formative critical workshop.
Among them are Hobsbaum and Lucie-Smith themselves, Peter
Porter, George MacBeth, Peter Redgrove and Alan Brownjohn. All
are represented in *A Group Anthology* (1963), along with David
Wevill, Taner Baybars and others, and even a solitary poem by
Adrian Mitchell, of whom later.

In a good essay on the Group, Roger Garfitt has written: 'As a
cultural encounter, its effects have not yet terminated; as a cultural
institution, there was a time-limit to its full effectiveness'. Edward
Lucie-Smith, in his foreword to *A Group Anthology,* said: 'The only
principle to which we would all subscribe is that poetry is
discussable . . . that the process by which words work in poetry is
something open to rational examination'. In a review of that book,
Alvarez commented that there was a Group preoccupation: 'It is
with, in one word, nastiness'. If there is a point at which these three
observations meet, I have not found it, nor indeed is it very useful
part-way through the 1980s to discuss as a phenomenon (other than
in Garfitt's historical terms) the possible unity of a caravan that has
passed on. I want instead to look at some of those who were once
members.

Peter Porter is in many ways the most successful of them, and his range and confidence have greatly expanded. In his first book (*Once Bitten Twice Bitten*, 1961) he seemed primarily a satirist, a fierce neo-Jacobean demolisher of social aspirations, the rich, the smug, the phoney, 'the smoothies of our Elizabethan age'. It was exhilaratingly unpleasant, but already it looks a bit dated:

> Cavalry-twilled tame publishers praising Logue,
> Classics Honours Men promoting Jazzetry.
>
> ('John Marston Advises Anger')

Such references will need footnotes before long. The satire has continued in successive books, but gradually Porter has emerged more solidly (and no less entertainingly) as an elegiac poet, with a sardonic approach to death and the things of the dead. He is a witty and exact namer of objects, and his poems are dense with them; but the effect of this is not to turn them into documentaries but fictions, so that sometimes they read like discontinuous parts of a huge verse novel, a *roman fleuve* of our time:

> Ten thousand unemployed are rioting
> The night your viola concerto's premiered.
> The light of diamonds speaks to your pale wits.
> 'I saw the host that sat and heard the king
> Speak to them on death. We will not be spared,
> Our country's a cold whore, a Grafenitz.'
>
> The town's on fire. The bombers will return.
> A priest brings round the late-night watered milk.
> The asylum clock ticks plainly in the dark.
> 'This is the sermon. Until our bodies burn
> God can't see us.' In your last silk
> Shirt by bomb light you are fingering Bach.
>
> ('Steps on the Way')

Porter has said that from the beginning his poems 'have polarized about the art and life of the past and the everyday world of the present'. In his work the Holy Roman Empire, John Cage, Bach, the experimental-ridiculous, advertising slogans, Cluny, Carthage, Beverly Hills and the Black Country co-exist, living parts of the continuous world of the imagination:

> God is a Super-Director
> who's terribly good at crowd scenes,
> but He has only one tense, the present.
> Think of pictures –
> Florentine or Flemish, with Christ
> or a saint – the softnesses of Luke,
> skulls of Golgotha, craftsmen's
> instruments of torture – everything is go!
>
> ('The Old Enemy')

Some of his most skilful work in this mingled area of past and present has been in his versions of Martial, the Roman poet of the first century AD. Porter has remodelled many of Martial's epigrams, freely using anachronism as a telescoping device in the cause of vividness and relevance:

> It's good to have a quiver-full of kids, Cinna,
>   even these days –
>   to hell with the population explosion,
>   your little woman's done a great job.
>   There's just one matter I'd mention,
>   none of them is yours!
> Nor your neighbours', nor your friends',
> nor the Elks', nor the Buffaloes', nor the Rotarians',
> nor even an overnight hippy's in the sleep-out!
>   You can tell this lot were mapped
>   on unmade morning beds or sliding mats.

Here's one with steel-wool hair;
a gift from Santra the Cook;

('After Martial', VI. xxxix)

Porter commands equally well mordantly colloquial inventions
('Your Attention Please', 'A Consumer's Report'), direct but more
formal and sententious pieces ('Seahorses', 'Fossil Gathering'), and
an exuberantly rough satirical mode, like a grinning death's-head,
shown in 'Applause for Death':

He's given a thousand Oxford lectures
And named a score of noble Hectors
Who left the earth like Hemingway
Lighter in animals for their stay;
His policy of defoliation
Gave Concrete Poetry to the nation;
His critical triumphs are recorded
In the ten books Leavis lauded
And he'll be there at the wheelwright's shop
When modernity shuffles to a stop . . .

This vein of satire is more playfully worked out in the second of his
two 'Poems with French Titles' (from *Preaching to the Converted*,
1972), 'Mort aux Chats', an amusing essay in rhetoric – the rhetoric
of prejudice and bigotry, whereby strong feelings are based on
misinformation, ignorance, intolerance, fear and hatred:

I blame my headache and my
plants dying on to cats.
Our district is full of them,
property values are falling.
When I dream of God I see
a Massacre of Cats. Why
should they insist on their own

language and religion, who
needs to purr to make his point?
Death to all cats! The Rule
of Dogs shall last a thousand years!

('Mort aux Chats')

All Porter's books have this element of satire, but for some time his
elegiac mode has been in the ascendant, particularly since *The Cost of
Seriousness* (1978). Some of the most moving poems in it, and in its
successor *English Subtitles* (1981), have their origin in the tragic early
death of his wife. 'An Exequy', deliberately written in the same
short-lined couplets as the famous elegy the seventeenth century
poet Henry King wrote for his own wife, is the most direct in its
tone:

The rooms and days we wandered through
Shrink in my mind to one – there you
Lie quite absorbed by peace – the calm
Which life could not provide is balm
In death. Unseen by me, you look
Past bed and stairs and half-read book
Eternally upon your home,
The end of pain, the left alone.

('An Exequy')

But Porter's range of reference has by no means diminished: high
art, rediscoveries of his native Australia (from which he moved to
London in 1951), annotations of Italy and the changing face of
Britain, are all fuel for his inventiveness and restless intelligence. The
Group perhaps gave him confidence in his earlier days to develop,
particularly in the direction of argumentative and even polemical
poems; but for many years his peculiar genius has been
self-propelled. His *Collected Poems* (1983) impressively gathers
together almost everything he has published since the early 1960s.

70

Another prolific and inventive member of the Group, admired (as Garfitt put it) for 'his versatility and panache', is George MacBeth. Right from the beginning, in the poems he published while he was an Oxford undergraduate in the early and mid-1950s, there has been an element of intellectual teasing in MacBeth, as if he deliberately courted an outraged or irritated response. The notion of provocative play, part of the force at work in his editing of the *Penguin Book of Sick Verse,* is exemplified in such earlier poems as 'Scissor-Man' and 'A True Story', through a great deal of *A Doomsday Book* (1965) – particularly in the 'poem-games', 'Fin du Globe' and 'The Ski Murders' – and is apparent throughout *The Orlando Poems* (1971), a sequence of poems which seems to take the open-ended structure of Ted Hughes's *Crow* but produces light squibs rather than smouldering grenades.

There has been a cheerful insolence about all this, but MacBeth's labelling of himself as 'the trapeze-artist of the abyss' is a typically ambiguous jest, toying with the genuine disturbances that seem to underlie much of his poetry. Sinister hints of diabolism, a relishing of sadism, violence, degradation, a preposterous flaunting of 'evil' – all these MacBeth characteristics can be seen as akin to the lurid paraphernalia employed by certain pop singers in their bid to win an easy notoriety. When he is at his most autobiographical, in such earlier poems as 'The Miner's Helmet' and 'The Drawer' and more recently in 'On the Death of May Street', there are no such extravagances and the manner is steadily grave, flatly undecorated:

So this dead, middle-aged, middle-class man
Killed by a misfired shell, and his wife
Dead of cirrhosis, have left one son
Aged nine, aged nineteen, aged twenty-six,
Who has buried them both in a cardboard box.

('The Drawer')

Contrast this with the fancifulness – what MacBeth has called 'the documentary surrealism' – of *A War Quartet* (1969), in which 'four turning-points of the Second World War' are embellished with a clogging verbosity:

> These
> And others would be in the mincer, tripped
> And fouled with slush and blood-rust in the bowl
> Before the year was out.
>   I chewed the rotten meat,
> Spitting.
>
>   ('At Stalingrad')

The distancing devices MacBeth uses are almost all of this baroque
sort, but sometimes they are more simply shocking, as in his
'distortions' of Keats's Odes. But these tactical failures shouldn't
obscure the fact that he can be straightforwardly comic, as in
'Painter's Model' and 'Dr Crippen's Elimination Kit', both of which
use cumulative or cataloguing devices to make their effect, and are
very accomplished light-satirical verse.

MacBeth's most recent collections, *Poems of Love and Death*
(1980), *Poems from Oby* (1982) and *The Long Darkness* (1983), are all
more sombre and more personally engaged than this. In particular,
Poems from Oby is an impressively unified book, almost entirely
drawing on his experience of the place in rural Norfolk to which he
withdrew in 1979 after many years of living in London and abroad.
Here he celebrates 'the luck of settlement, finding a piece of land to
feel secure on, and someone to live there with':

> I walk tonight through silence, and watch smoke
> Circle above the chimneys of your aims
> In quiet air; and, hearing the far stroke
> Of human axes, I renounce cold games
>
> As my intent; and, by the sound of blades
> Through fallen wood, at distance, I defer
> To country ease.
>
>   ('This Evening, Lisa')

The directness and tenderness of this is typical of MacBeth's latest poems, and in their technical as well as their personal confidence they mark a satisfying maturity, not needing tricks on the trapeze to win an audience.

Peter Redgrove studied science at Cambridge, and behind a good deal of his work there is the sense of a passionate scientist, someone who understands the physical laws of the universe but who at the same time sees them as a kind of magic. Redgrove has an imaginative richness which sometimes looks wildly eccentric, mystical and comic at once. Some of his poems seem to hold an enormous magnifying glass up to Nature, so that the uprooting of a daisy appears a labour of the same magnitude as the felling of a mighty oak; they can boil with an energy that is too muscle bound:

> I sit in the hot room and I sweat . . .
> And those wet red blooms like sliced tomatoes –
> I want to get in there with a thick insulting stick . . .

In his earlier work, Redgrove was seen to be something of the same sort of writer as Ted Hughes; but though both Hughes and Redgrove are possibly romantic soothsayers, and though their inspiration can often be seen as basically irrational – in fact basically *anti*-rational – Redgrove has become a more careful organizer of language than Hughes, at least in his more recent manifestations. The early prose-poem monologues, such as 'Mr Waterman' and 'The Sermon', were successful grotesque inventions which had an imposed dramatic form. More recent poems, such as 'The Idea of Entropy at Maenporth Beach', have a beautifully intense gracefulness mixed with the grotesquerie:

> She laughs aloud, and bares her teeth again, and cries:
> Now that I am all black, and running in my richness . . .
> And knowing it a little, I shall take great care
> To keep a little black about me somewhere.
> A snotty nostril, a mourning nail will do.
> Mud is a good dress, but not the best.

Ah, watch, she runs into the sea. She walks
In streaky white on dazzling sands that stretch
Like the whole world's pursy mud unpurged.

('The Idea of Entropy at Maenporth Beach')

Some of Alan Brownjohn's poems, such as 'Snow in Bromley' and
'We are going to see the rabbit' (from *The Railings,* 1961), became
small classics of social comment, but his has been a very gradually
achieved reputation. *Warrior's Career,* published in 1972 when he was
forty, was the first really to show his range of techniques and
sympathies, in particular in some cross-sections of invented human
relationships. Brownjohn himself has said that a number of his
poems tend towards 'the condition of fiction', almost as situations or
incidents from a novel or short story: characters are revealed
obliquely or through their own monologues – a girl disc-jockey, a
smart young executive, salesmen and antique dealers and politicians.
There were many of these in *A Song of Good Life* (1975) and more
again in *A Night in the Gazebo* (1980). Some are light, such as
'Especially' and the group of poems centring on a character called
'The Old Fox', an ingenious rogue; but most show a mingling of
acute human observation with a basic melancholy, so that even the
ridiculous or the reprehensible (as in the hotel managers in the
title-poem of *A Night in the Gazebo*) are touched with sadness:

Lastly, gaze out there at the crematorium.
    Having consumed fourteen
Tequilas in half-an-hour, a manager
Is being consumed to rest. His wife comes first,
And behind her follow forty-six girls in all,
The youngest sixteen, the oldest thirty-four,
And all in states of nostalgia or raw distress
According to how lately they knew the man.
So wife and girls compassionate each other
As the clergyman, noting an ancient English
Ritual of mourning, shakes each girl by the hand.
If this can happen, the world must be good. It is ten forty-five.

Brownjohn's *Collected Poems 1952–83* (1984) demonstrate his quiet mastery.

Edwin Brock is another poet of social comment; he too was an attender of the Group, though he is not represented in *A Group Anthology*. His ironies are usually more straightforwardly presented than Brownjohn's, and they make neatly devastating points about violence and heartlessness: e.g. two of his best-known poems, 'Five Ways to Kill a Man' and 'Song of the Battery Hen'. This second title became the title of his 'Selected Poems 1959–1975':

> We can't grumble about accommodation:
> we have a new concrete floor that's
> always dry, four walls that are
> painted white, and a sheet-iron roof
> the rain drums on. A fan blows warm air
> beneath our feet to disperse the smell
> of chickenshit and, on dull days,
> fluorescent lighting sees us.
>
>   ('Song of the Battery Hen')

Through a great deal of Brock's work runs a common thread of supple, sometimes apparently artless but always direct and colloquial examination and self-examination. The manner is doggedly honest, touched with humorous self-deprecation:

> These are my credentials:
> I am clever
> and I am aware.
>
> You buy me
> in a small transparent ball
> almost entirely filled with water.
> You shake me
> and a plastic snowstorm
> will ensue.
>
>   ('A Man of the World')

The later poems, often concerned with both the loving intimacy and the precariousness of family life, use natural imagery – rivers, trees, cows, herons – as a counterpoint to what is actually an urban, as well as urbane, sense of poise. Nothing can quite banish his disquiet:

> Truly these trees twist us with a hint
> of roots. I do not understand why
> a concern for others is our responsibility
> or God's. Only this is planned:
> that we will grow vegetables, watching
> week by week the soil reveal its hand.
> That, and our rotting compost heap.
>
> ('These trees')

One could point to good individual poems by other one-time members of the Group (Edward Lucie Smith's 'The Lime Tree', 'The Lesson' and 'The Link'; Philip Hobsbaum's 'The Intellectual at Thorne'; Martin Bell's 'Letter to a Friend' and some of his 'Don Senilio' sequence), and to other poets who, without associating with the Group, have shared some of its manners and concerns, domestic and social: Brian Jones's poems of tender and troubled family life; Jon Stallworthy's moving sequence on the birth of a mongol child, 'The Almond Tree', and on his ancestry in 'A Familiar Tree'; and – from a vast and over-reaching output – the best work of an older man, David Holbrook, who through years of obsessive polemical prose about what he regards as the *trahison des clercs* in matters of sexual morals has gone on producing some finely observed poems about married love, stress and growth, often seen in terms of growing and dying nature.

Since the Group dispersed later in the 1960s, a number of poets have followed on who can be seen to relate to it, including some (such as Fleur Adcock and Jenny Joseph) who were already publishing widely at the time the Group was in existence, but who have established their individuality since. Fleur Adcock is elegant and colloquial, astringent, ironical: such poems as 'Future Work' and 'Against Coupling' are both fastidious and funny, and the directly personal, even anecdotal origins of her poems are mediated in a cool but not unfeeling way. The edges of Jenny Joseph's poems are often rougher, her tone of voice less obviously controlled and urbane: the title of her book *The Thinking Heart* (1978) points towards her concerns, which may at first seem to be accurate but casual annotations of daily domestic life but which later take on some of the quality of parables.

11

Freda Downie, U.A. Fanthorpe, Elma Mitchell, Vicki Feaver, Carol Rumens, E.J. Scovell

Mention of Fleur Adcock and Jenny Joseph is a reminder that the 1970s and 1980s have seen a great deal of activity among women poets. Some of this activity has been quite self-consciously part of the 'women's movement', the 'feminism', of these years, in anthologies of women's poetry and in general in the area of protest and polemics. But the best poems, as always, tend to come from individuals, not groups or movements; and this is undoubtedly true of the work of not only Fleur Adcock and Jenny Joseph but also that of Freda Downie, U.A. Fanthorpe, Elma Mitchell, Vicki Feaver and Carol Rumens.

They have distinct voices. Freda Downie often looks at familiar things quizzically (a pair of gloves, a pan of fish, a chair, a spider), or uses moments of fancy or fantasy in a way that is both matter-of-fact and surprising:

> I thought you were nothing
> More than a dry stain that is
> Found on the page of a book
> Where once an insect,
> Having reached a certain line,
> Was crushed to death
> By the reader.
>
> But histories never
> Properly confined you.
> Daily you make your mark
> On wide news-sheets.
> Your hood is off,

You display your teeth.
Like the shirt on your back,
They are in good repair.

('Torturer')★

U.A. Fanthorpe in some of her poems draws on her daily life as a hospital clerk, but she too is a witty and compassionate recorder of a wider range of everyday life ('Carol Concert', 'Men on Allotments'), and in the title poem of her book *Side Effects* (or rather in the poem which obliquely refers to it, 'Not My Best Side') produced a marvellously funny triptych based on Uccello's painting 'St George and the Dragon', in which dragon, maiden and saint in turn speak of their feelings.

Elma Mitchell, Vicki Feaver and Carol Rumens perhaps tend to speak more self-consciously as women. Elma Mitchell's 'Thoughts after Ruskin' is particularly inventive and clear-eyed:

Women reminded him of lilies and roses.
Me they remind rather of blood and soap,
Armed with a warm rag, assaulting noses,
Ears, neck, mouth and all the secret places:

Armed with a sharp knife, cutting up liver,
Holding hearts to bleed under a running tap,
Gutting and stuffing, pickling and preserving,
Scalding, blanching, broiling, pulverising,
– All the terrible chemistry of their kitchens.

('Thoughts after Ruskin')

Vicki Feaver's poems, collected in *Close Relatives* (1981), are mainly concerned with the tensions and pleasures of ordinary domestic life: husbands and wives, mothers and children, children in relation to their parents. The poems are very clear, tender, touched with wistfulness and pathos:

Sometimes I have wanted
to throw you off
like a heavy coat.

Sometimes I have said
you would not let me
breathe or move.

But now that I am free
to choose light clothes
or none at all

I feel the cold
and all the time I think
how warm it used to be.

('Coat')★

Carol Rumens can be as nakedly direct as this, but also tougher and
more sophisticated, in some poems ('The Witch's Manuscript',
'Charlotte's Journey', 'Akhmatova in Leningrad') identifying with
women in extreme situations:

Cover me, seas of singing, stop my heart
and throat before another night's command.
In darkness, every world's a furious brand
that lights an ankle-snapping fire. I mount
black clouds and ride upon a storm of cries,
hugging a stick as red claws reach my thighs.

('The Witch's Manuscript')

An older poet whose most recent work appeared after what seemed
to be a long silence is E.J. Scovell. She is of the Auden generation,
though her earliest books did not come out until the 1940s, and after
the highly-praised *The River Steamer* (1956) there was nothing in

book form until *The Space Between* (1982). The new poems show the same immaculate grace and penetrating poignancy as the earlier ones:

If to die should be so –
To hear: 'It is a dream; let it go' and loose as we must
The unknown that's all we know –
Even in oblivion I should mourn a whole world lost.
Signs dark to understand, pearls never dived for yet
I should find means to regret.

('A Dream Forgotten')

12

Geoffrey Hill, Jon Silkin, Charles Tomlinson, Basil Bunting, Roy Fisher

'Experiment' in poetry is an unsatisfactorily elastic term, and is indifferently applied to writers who have drawn on foreign models (whether American or non-English language), to those who in some sense have re-used the manners and materials of the early twentieth-century modernists, and to others who have moved into areas where the visual arts and music are supposed to merge with poetry. I shall deal with the third of these later in the present essay. For the moment I want to look at a number of poets who have been rightly or wrongly labelled as experimental, perhaps because they have not seemed to fit into any easily recognizable English niche: in his Penguin anthology *British Poetry Since 1945*, Edward Lucie-Smith puts one of them (Basil Bunting) under the heading 'Sources', another (Jon Silkin) is placed among 'Expressionists', and the rest (Geoffrey Hill, Charles Tomlinson, Roy Fisher) are said to have been subject to 'Influences from Abroad'. Clearly such pigeon-holing is arbitrary, but I can't volunteer anything better.

'Influences from Abroad' would be particularly hard to track down in much of the work of Geoffrey Hill, the topography of whose poems is peculiarly English and whose sense of history touches on many specifically English events. His dense, formal, formidable poems have gradually established themselves, though he is still much less well known than he should be among ordinary readers of poetry. It is in the estimate of other poets that he stands particularly high – for example, in the answers to a 1972 questionnaire sent out by *the Review* to many poets and critics, the poet most often mentioned as a hopeful sign was Hill, specifically on the strength of his *Merican Hymns* (1971). But *Mercian Hymns* – one of the finest achievements during the period with which this essay deals – did not appear from nowhere: its roots can be seen in *For the Unfallen* (1959) and *King Log* (1968).

Hill's deeply serious concerns and the ceremonial exactness of

Geoffrey Hill

his language were already apparent in poems written before he was twenty – in 'Genesis', 'Holy Thursday' and 'God's Little Mountain':

Below, the river scrambled like a goat
Dislodging stones. The mountain stamped its foot,
Shaking, as from a trance. And I was shut
With wads of sound into a sudden quiet.

('God's Little Mountain')

These early poems, later collected in *For the Unfallen,* have an ample but severely controlled rhetoric which he continued to master. There is a rapt sense of struggle for exactness, for the precise word which will also be the resonant word: 'Where fish at dawn ignite the powdery lake'. *King Log* took the process much further, so that sometimes the taut compression becomes congestion, a tight-lipped ritualistic speech impressive in its gestures but not offering a ready key:

Anguish bloated by the replete scream.
Flesh of abnegation: the poem
Moves grudgingly to its extreme form,

Vulnerable, to the lamp's fierce head
Of well-trimmed light. In darkness outside,
Foxes and rainsleeked stones and the dead –

Aliens of such a theme – endure
Until I could cry 'Death! Death!' as though
To exacerbate that suave power';. . .

('Three Baroque Meditations')

The two substantial sequences in *King Log* – 'Funeral Music' and 'The Songbook of Sebastian Arrurruz' – show distinct contrasts both in theme and in the way Hill uses compressed and chiselled language. 'Funeral Music' consists of eight fourteen-line poems suggested by bloody incidents during the fifteenth-century Wars of the Roses: an attempt, as Hill has characteristically commented, at 'a florid grim music broken by grunts and shrieks':

> They bespoke doomsday and they meant it by
> God, their curved metal rimming the low ridge.
> But few appearances are like this. Once
> Every five hundred years a comet's
> Over-riding stillness might reveal men
> In such array, livid and featureless,
> With England crouched beastwise beneath it all.
> 'Oh, that old northern business . . .' A field
> After battle utters its own sound
> Which is like nothing on earth, but is earth.
> Blindly the questing snail, vulnerable
> Mole emerge, blindly we lie down, blindly
> Among carnage the most delicate souls
> Tup in their marriage-blood, gasping 'Jesus'.

The brooding sombreness of this is not simply pitying and elegiac: it is laced through with ironies, each phrase is delicately poised to re-create (without loose atmospherics or over-colourful images) a precise and horrible scene, of scrupulous interest in itself and beyond itself; a sound 'Which is like nothing on earth, but is earth'. In an early essay on Hill's work ('Cliché as "Responsible Speech"'), Christopher Ricks demonstrated the way in which Geoffrey Hill uses casual phrases and dead metaphors so that they are 'rinsed and restored', as 'like nothing on earth' is treated in the line just quoted. The 'grim music' of this sequence is orchestrated in this fashion, and the effect is both massive and finely sensitive.

'The Songbook of Sebastian Arrurruz' is a more fragmentary and oblique group which 'represents the work of an apocryphal Spanish poet' – a device which distances but does not coldly objectify moods of regret and sexual desolation: bitterness, loss, hopeless sensuality conflict:

There would have been things to say, quietness
That could feed on our lust, refreshed
Trivia, the occurrences of the day;
And at night my tongue in your furrow.

Without you I am mocked by courtesies
And chat, where satisfied women push
Dutifully toward some unneeded guest
Desirable features of conversation.

('From the Latin')★

But the poems are not just fictions about a former passion: they are
themselves embodiments of the strategies to which a poet is forced
when he grapples with his material and turns it into art, finding how
(as William Empson once put it) to 'learn a style from a despair'.

The thirty prose poems that make up *Mercian Hymns* centre on
the eighth-century King of the West-Midlands, Offa, but the effort
here is not towards the re-creation of the past as it was with 'Funeral
Music'. The commanding and unifying figure is sometimes the
ancient king, sometimes the poet himself in childhood or present
manhood: throughout the sequence, the remote past, the recent past
and the present are obliquely presented, often within the space of a
single section – as is plain from the beginning:

King of the perennial holly-groves, the riven sand-
stone: overlord of the M5: architect of the historic
rampart and ditch, the citadel at Tamworth, the
summer hermitage in Holy Cross: guardian of the
Welsh Bridge and the Iron Bridge: contractor to
the desirable new estates: saltmaster: money-
changer: commissioner for oaths: martyrologist:
the friend of Charlemagne

'I liked that,' said Offa, 'sing it again.'

('Mercian Hymns I')★

If *Mercian Hymns* has any stylistic source other than the historical sources to which Hill's notes make droll and learned references, it may be partly in St-John Perse's *Anabasis,* which T.S. Eliot translated and published in 1931, and partly in David Jones (see pp. 5-7); but really the method and tone are like nothing else in English – complex, rich, many-layered, an intricately worked meditation on history, tradition, order, power and memory, in which the precision of the language and the mysterious reverberations of the past combine to achieve something completely inevitable and true:

'Now when King Offa was alive and dead', they were
    all there, the funereal gleemen: papal legate and
    rural dean; Merovingian car-dealers, Welsh mercen-
    aries; a shuffle of house-carls.

He was defunct. They were perfunctory. The ceremony
    stood acclaimed. The mob received memorial vouchers
    and signs.

After that shadowy, thrashing midsummer hail-storm,
    Earth lay for a while, the ghost-bride of livid
    Thor, butcher of strawberries, and the shire-tree
    dripped red in the arena of its uprooting.

('Mercian Hymns XXVII')★

Hill's book *Tenebrae* (1978) returned to the strict forms of his work before *Mercian Hymns*: it also bears out – though after the event – Lucie-Smith's labelling 'Influences from Abroad', in that the opening sequence, 'The Pentecost Castle', draws on old Spanish songs (*coplas*) of sacred and profane love, and others have their points of departure in German poems. But the main body of the book, made up of the sonnet-sequences 'Lachrimae' and 'An Apology for the Revival of Christian Architecture in England', relates much more to English devotional and meditative models, with a majestic reverberance that sometimes reminds one of Crashaw, sometimes of Tennyson, but so hammered and turned that they could be by no one but Hill:

Autumn resumes the land, ruffles the woods
with smoky wings, entangles them. Trees shine
out from their leaves, rocks mildew to moss-green;
the avenues are spread with brittle floods.

Platonic England, house of solitudes,
rests in its laurels and its injured stone,
replete with complex fortunes that are gone,
beset by dynasties of moods and clouds.

It stands, as though at ease with its own world,
the mannerly extortions, languid praise,
all that devotion long since bought and sold,
the rooms of cedar and soft-thudding baize,
tremulous boudoirs where the crystals kissed
in cabinets of amethyst and frost.

('The Laurel Axe': from 'An Apology for the Revival of Christian
Architecture in England')★

Hill's *The Mystery of the Charity of Charles Péguy* (1983) is a long,
allusive meditation, written in sonorous quatrains, on the
implications of the life and death of the French poet, and it has been
acutely called 'an oblique autobiography of the spirit'.

Jon Silkin has written one of the most extensive appraisals of Hill's
work, but there are few resemblances between them. Silkin's early
poems were like emblematic versions of D.H. Lawrence, and the
contest between a heavily didactic element and something much
more spontaneous and visceral has continued. But the didactic or
moralizing stuff almost disappears in the sequence of 'Flower
Poems' (in *Nature With Man*), first published in 1964, which fix
concentratedly on the individualities of plants and flowers, using
separate curt statements to build up a whole:

The rootless strawberry plant
Moves across the soil. It hops
Six inches. Has no single location,

Or root.
You cannot point to its origin,
Or parent. It shoots out
A pipe, and one more plant
Consolidates its ground.
It puts out crude petals, loosely met.
As if the business of flowering
Were to be got over . . .

('The Strawberry Plant')

The dogged seriousness of Silkin's concerns (about man's injustice
and cruelty, for example) often seem to weigh his poems down with
urgently meant but inert abstractions, and in general his admirers
appear to be impressed by the gravity of his intentions rather than the
actual results.

A much more detached observer – in many ways an aesthete – is
Charles Tomlinson. Many of his poems are highly organized pieces
of visual perception, the work of a man who is also a painter and
graphic artist. In his early poems the perceptions were filtered
through the style of Wallace Stevens, but Tomlinson is eclectic – one
might more rudely say that he is a bit of a cultural magpie – and he
has gone on to use some of the manners of William Carlos Williams
and such Spanish, French and Russian poets as he has translated.
Certainly he seems to have little sympathy with anything (other than
Hill's *Mercian Hymns*) that passes for poetry in England today; his
reputation was first made in the United States, and still stands
highest there, though he has devoted disciples in Britain too. I find
myself repelled by the arid fastidiousness of much of Tomlinson's
work, and too often find asceticism and scratchiness where the aim
was perhaps towards sensuousness and opulence, or marginal
comment evading confrontation, as in

Too little
has been said
of the door, its one
face turned to the night's

downpour and its other
to the shift and glisten of firelight.

('The Door')

And even when Tomlinson satisfactorily captures a richer fancy
he is apt to let it go in empty surmise, as in the fourth and fifth
stanzas of 'The Fox': he finds the corpse of a fox in the snow:

Domed at the summit, then tapering,
the drift still mocked
my mind as if the whole
fox-infested hill were the skull of a fox.

Scallops and dips
of pure pile rippled and shone, but what
should I do with such beauty
eyed by that?

Ezra Pound's most loyal British follower has been Basil Bunting,
who in the 1960s emerged from neglect to become in his own right a
father-figure and symbol to some poets in this country. *The Spoils*
(1965), *Briggflatts* (1966) and his *Collected Poems* (1978) all have a
gritty hieratic resonance, much of which comes from a Poundian
mingling of proper names: his native Northumberland is juxtaposed
with the sonorities of the Near East or Italy, and harshness is played
off against mellifluousness:

Under his right oxter the loom of his sweep
the pilot turns from the wake.
Thole-pins shred where the oar leans,
grommets renewed, tallowed;
halliards frapped to the shrouds.

('Briggflatts')

But with this riot of rare and tasty vocabulary one sometimes has the sneaking suspicion that (in Bunting's own words from *Briggflatts*)

It looks well on the page, but never
well enough.

Bunting's real standing seems to be that of someone who has survived with lonely integrity: the work itself has little obvious relationship with that of his young champions, such as Tom Pickard and Barry MacSweeney, and its own indebtedness to Pound – though it is much more available and palatable than the Pound of the *Cantos* – makes it seem doubtful pastiche, right down to the harsh, rasping manner in which Bunting recites it. Like Charles Tomlinson, Bunting's most enthusiastic reception has been in America, where the so-called Black Mountain movement constructed a whole cookery-book of experimental precept and practice in the wake of Ezra Pound and William Carlos Williams. Charles Olson and Robert Creeley are key American names in this area, and they have a certain incoherent and fragmented following in Britain.

Among British poets one could cite here are Roy Fisher, Tom Raworth, Lee Harwood, and Jeremy Prynne. Roy Fisher is the least Americanized of them. His *The Ship's Orchestra* (1966) is an hallucinated prose-poem which has something of the static concentrated descriptiveness of the French anti-novel: incidents and actions are written of repetitively as if in slow motion. His *Collected Poems* (1981) contains some shorter pieces which use the same technique, as in 'The Small Room':

Why should I let him shave the hairs from me? I hardly know
him.

Of all the rooms, this is a very small room.

I cannot tell if it was he who painted the doors this colour;
himself who lit the fire just before I arrived.

That bulb again. It has travelled even here.

In the corner, a cupboard where evidently a dog sleeps. The
preparations are slow.

Less wearisome than this are some of the parts of the 'City' sequence,
which uses cinematic techniques of scanning movement and close-
up to present an urban landscape: the device is at least as old as the
1920s – a remark one could make with some asperity of much work
considered experimental today – but there are greyly atmospheric
moments.

13

'Concrete', 'Sound', 'Found':
Edwin Morgan, Bob Cobbing

A more obviously extreme experimentalism has been concerned, in Britain as elsewhere, with forms of visual and aural presentation which treat words as objects for display. These are international phenomena. Concrete poetry, it has been said by the American Eugene Wildman, 'aims, in general, at the ideogrammatic state': so it is natural that the Japanese, whose basic written language is ideogrammatic, have been active in the field. The appeal to Czechs, Brazilians, Germans, and indeed British, is less obvious, but the notion of a poetry that can immediately transcend all linguistic barriers is of course a seductive one. Whether it can be of more than peripheral importance is another matter.

The modern origins of concrete poetry can be found in the work of such artists as Arp and Kandinsky, and in the pioneers of Dadaism, such as Tzara. The idea began to establish itself in Britain a good deal later: its recent exponents have included John Furnival, Dom Sylvester Houédard, Ian Hamilton Finlay, Edwin Morgan and Alan Riddell. Their approaches vary. Some construct a 'treated' text – that is, a cut-up process using words already printed and dislocating them to make new patterns. Others choose to make letters of different sizes and colours within a carefully organized space, often in the form of a poster, and here the effect is almost entirely pictorial. Some use a typewriter as if it were a picture-making device, others to make verbal and visual puns. There seems to be a strong element of play in all this – but no doubt these exponents would argue that that is an essential part of all poetry-making.

Within the limits of conventional typesetting it is difficult to illustrate much of this sort of thing, but there are regular publications entirely devoted to it. Edwin Morgan, a Scottish writer who has also published some good 'conventional' poems, is one of the most inventive and witty experimentalists: some of his work seems to blend both concrete and sound characteristics, as in his 'Chinese Cat'★:

```
pmrkgniaou
pmrkgniao
pmrkniao
pmrniao
pmriao
pmiao
miao
mao
```

Another of Morgan's inventions takes a famous poem by the seventeenth-century Japanese poet Basho and turns it into a 'Summer Haiku'★:

```
    Pool.
   Peopl
    e  plop!
   Cool.
```

Sound poetry, which performs similar acts of dislocation on spoken language, has gone hand in hand with the development of the tape-recorder – though of course Apollinaire and others produced work which shares something with both concrete and sound many years before that machine was invented. The most indefatigable figure in this area in Britain is Bob Cobbing. The American Robert Lax and the German Ernst Jandl have been closely associated with him, and much of their work is available on records. In his earlier work, such as 'An ABC in Sound', Cobbing relied solely on the variations of the untreated human voice. His note to the following piece★ observes, 'French words pronounced as French, English as English. Make the most of each consonant and vowel':

```
Bombast bombast
Bomb bomb bomb bast
Bombast
Emphase
```

Em- em- em- phase
Bombast emphase
Bombast
Phébus

With the tape-recorded pieces, different levels and speeds of sound are used, together with extraneous, non-human and sometimes electronic elements, so that the result is often indistinguishable from *musique concrète*. Most of Cobbing's recent poems exist only on tape.

These experiments, usually in their simpler forms, have from time to time been used by poets whose work is generally untouched by such considerations: George MacBeth's 'Pavan for an Unborn Infanta' and his 'vowel and numerical analyses' are examples. The phenomenon of the 'found poem' has similarly been occasionally taken up, as in Alan Brownjohn's 'Found under Capricorn' and 'Common Sense'. The 'found poem' uses already existing prose material (a newspaper item, or – in the case of the Brownjohn poems – extracts from horoscope columns in women's magazines and problems in an old arithmetic book) and brings out its latent ironies by isolating, juxtaposing or shuffling the component parts. This is what Henry Graham and James Mangnall have done with picture captions from *Time* magazine:

In the wild fake jungle of beard, an authentic spark.
Two halves of a popsicle, two cats in a sack;
Joan of Arc and Lolita –
from saintmanship to supreme anxiety,
from cannibalism to consecration.

('A Faceful of Agnostic Pie')

The argument for these pieces is that all art involves a process of selection, of choosing from a given set of materials, and that, in his choice of an already existing group of words and his detachment of their intended meaning, the poet has 'made' his own poem. Sometimes (as in John Daniel's use of philosophical texts) the poet is totally faithful to his original to the extent that he changes nothing;

others extrapolate from the selected material and are thus more open in their own attitude – as in Peter Porter's 'Pig in the Middle', which plays only slightly exaggerated tricks with a publicity news–item about a luxuriously reared pig, but enough to underline the ludicrousness of the event on which it is commenting.

Concrete and sound poetry have their dedicated and serious practitioners, and though my own attitude is that such work is culturally marginal it deserves to be treated with something other than contempt: it is a sign of *homo ludens,* and its ingenuities are sometimes genuinely mind-stretching. Found poetry, at least in its simplest manifestations, seems more dubious, or less serious in its implied function. The aim of all these devotees is inclusivism, which at its most extreme expresses itself as: 'Art is whatever I say it is'. This is dangerous doctrine in the mouths of untalented or boring men, and it is a peculiarly modern one. 'Divisions between the arts are breaking down', as Bob Cobbing has written: to some, the contemplation of destruction is itself a form of enjoyment – even a form of art – though in a century that has seen as much destruction as ours such tastes should surely be repugnant.

14

'The Review' and after:
Ian Hamilton, A. Alvarez,
Hugo Williams, David Harsent

A good many of the topics and poets touched on in this essay were the continuous subject of appraisal, demolition and contempt in a magazine which began life towards the start of my time-period: *the Review*. Founded by Ian Hamilton in 1962, it celebrated its tenth anniversary in 1972 with a special issue to which I have already referred, before metamorphosing into a much larger literary periodical, the *New Review*, which existed notably and controversially until 1978. *The Review*'s spiritual ancestor was clearly Geoffrey Grigson's *New Verse,* in its combativeness, its scalpel-like intelligence, its rough or sly humour, and even – initially – its neat and rather austere format. But, though concerned wholly with poetry, it was not notably generous in the space allotted to poems themselves – a contrast here with *New Verse,* in which Grigson published a more catholic choice of poems than one might have supposed from reading his strictures and dismissals elsewhere in the magazine. The narrow acerbities of *the Review* had an effect that went far beyond its small circulation, but chiefly in the arena of controversy. Those who admired it might say that its main concern was to keep up standards: those who disliked it, that it was brutally destructive and almost wholly negative.

Yet something like a *Review* school of poets was noticed, with Ian Hamilton as its chief representative, A. Alvarez as its *éminence grise* (Edna Longley, in an unsympathetic essay, called Alvarez 'the group's conscience'), and David Harsent and Hugo Williams among its rank-and-file. (But one ought to point out that *the Review* also gave space to poems by such writers as Douglas Dunn, James Fenton, John Fuller, Peter Dale and Jon Stallworthy, none of whom can be characterized by the descriptions that follow; and, with the *New Review,* the net was extended, carrying much work by Clive James, for example.)

Of his own poems, Ian Hamilton has written that

> they could all, I suppose, be described as
> dramatic lyrics. That is to say, the reader
> is offered only the intense, climactic moment
> of a drama – the prose part, the part which
> provides the background data, is left to the
> imagination.

His only full-length book so far is *The Visit* (1970), which drew on eight years work. The crises, or 'climactic moments', with which the poems deal are isolated vignettes of dying or death, of mental stress or breakdown, in which the poet is not at the centre of the event but its concerned observer, tied by blood or affection, resigned to hopelessness or guilt. In their brevity (several of them are only six or seven lines long) the poems seem almost refined beyond reticence, stripped down to something so taciturn as to be practically silent, as in 'Curfew'*:

> It's midnight
> And our silent house is listening
> To the last sounds of people going home.
> We lie beside our curtained window
> Wondering
> What makes them do it.

The risks of evanescent portentousness in this sort of thing are great, as are the dangers of threadbare banality. But read as a whole, *The Visit* makes a considerable impact: the discontinuous threads become almost a plain spool of narrative – that 'prose part' Hamilton referred to. And the best of them can stand perfectly well on their own:

> Four weathered gravestones tilt against the wall
> Of your Victorian asylum.
> Out of bounds, you kneel in the long grass

Deciphering obliterated names:
Old lunatics who died here.

('Memorial')★

Among the others associated with Hamilton, Alvarez is one of the most interesting. A meagrely productive poet, his early verses of the 1950s are generally consummate pieces of Empsonian pastiche, the most intelligent of their kind, but they look like exhibits now, not living works of art. It was during the 1960s that he wrote a handful of tense poems that are more fully fleshed out than the typical *Review* minimalisms. Such a poem as 'Back' (about an attempt at suicide) is clinical and almost documentary in its presentation:

Was it the *tremor mortis,* the last dissolution
Known now in dreams, unknown in the pit itself
When I was gripped by the neck till my life shook
Like loosening teeth in my head? Yet I recall
Nothing of death but the puzzled look on your face,
Swimming towards me, weeping, clouded, uncertain,
As they took the tube from my arm
And plugged the strange world back in place.

Hugo Williams was so thoroughly held in thrall for a time by Hamiltonian minimalism that he seemed to produce nothing but fragile pastiche (though such poems as 'Sugar Daddy' and 'The Butcher' escaped it). More recently he has written much more confidently and extensively, drawing directly on his own upbringing as the child of rich and slightly bohemian theatre-folk, and the results have been much better. David Harsent, too, after years of looking like a standard *Review* copyist, full of *angst* and effortful aridity, has in the past few years written some tougher, harder-edged poems which have a sophisticated poise which is more individual. Rather like the case of the Group, the *Review* school seems to have split up into a number of individuals, with the strongest talents surviving and growing.

15

'Pop' and after:
Christopher Logue, Adrian Mitchell, Adrian Henri, Roger McGough, Brian Patten, Pete Morgan

As I said at the beginning of this survey, I find myself now taking an historical view of that phenomenon of the 1960s and early 1970s, 'pop' poetry. Like such disparate contemporary happenings as the rise of the Beatles, the transatlantic popularity of Leonard Cohen, Rod McKuen and Bob Dylan, and the television satire of 'That Was the Week That Was', it is beginning to have an almost period charm. In my 1973 version, I described Christopher Logue and Adrian Mitchell as 'two immediate forebears' of the pop poets, and that is still the way they look. Now that their progeny have themselves come into perspective, it may be possible to consider all of them more coolly and objectively.

Christopher Logue's Brechtian poems from *Songs* (1959) still look accomplished and attractive: 'The Story about the Road', 'The Song of the Dead Soldier', 'The Ass's Song', 'Various Rules'. His versions of Homer's *Ilia – Patrocleia* (1962) and *Pax* (1967) – have been expanded into a dramatic work, *War Music,* which has been staged, broadcast and televised successfully. His shorter poems have appeared more sporadically, and he no longer seems to be at the centre of the satirical stage, having as his main platform nowadays the column in *Private Eye* magazine, 'True Stories', in which he garners and processes bizarre news-items from the world's press.

Adrian Mitchell's *Poems* (1964) and *Out Loud* (1968) are worth going back to both for their humanitarianism and their humour. His classic piece of satire, frequently anthologized and rightly so, is 'The Oxford Hysteria of English Poetry', a hilarious encapsulation of the life of the bard from the Stone Age to the present day:

Then suddenly – WOOMF –
It was the Ro-man-tic Re-viv-al
And it didn't matter how you wrote,
All the public wanted was a hairy great image.
Before they'd even print you
You had to smoke opium, die of consumption,
Fall in love with your sister
And drown in the Mediterranean (not at Brighton).
My publisher said: 'I'll have to remainder you
Unless you go and live in a lake or something
Like this bloke Wordsworth.'

The nature of Mitchell's protest poetry, as in

My brain socialist
My heart anarchist
My eyes pacifist
My blood revolutionary

('Loose Leaf Poem')

now looks very mild compared with the 'rants' of John Cooper
Clark, Linton Kwesi Johnson and 'Attila the Stockbroker', whom I
mentioned earlier. They have emerged from a bitterly anti- or
non-literary sub-stratum, which can be suspicious of Mitchell's
middle-class, university origins, for all his warm-heartedness and
anti-establishmentarianism.

The Liverpool poets, headed by Adrian Henri, Roger McGough
and Brian Patten, reached a very wide and mainly young audience in
the late 1960s and early 1970s, partly through such anthologies as
The Liverpool Scene, The Mersey Sound and *Children of Albion,* partly
through their frequent appearances on stages throughout the
country and on television. With such practice over many years, all
three are now old troupers, and they must rely on surefire audience-
holding techniques, not on the charm or self-identification of mere

youth: after all, Henri was born in 1932, McGough in 1937, and even Patten (born 1946) is not the young colt he once was. With all of them, what survives best, and what they continue to produce most effectively, is comical verse. Henri's sentimental love rhapsodies, even Patten's dreamy urban fantasies, have receded into the decade that brought them forth.

Pete Morgan, who emerged a little later with *The Grey Mare Being the Better Steed* (1973), produced in his 'Meat Work Saga' an impressive 'pop' performance which was reinforced in other parts of that book. At his best he has a quite exceptional sophisticated control and attack, which developed in *The Spring Collection* (1979). These poems are by turns humorous, melancholy, impudent, and tenderly lyrical, sometimes with a nervous cutting edge:

> To set the table in a roar –
> To contemplate the devil's vest.
>
> The life of the party –
> The soul of the queue.
>
> Brave to the backbone –
> Full of wince.
>
> To wallow in the mire –
> To hold your own.
>
> Out of the wood –
> And into the midden.
>
> Never say die –
> Say panic.
>
> ('Six Secret Slogans')★

Now that poetry readings are a commonplace in Britain, the impact of the peripatetic poet appearing in front of audiences large and small has probably become diffused. 'A sacramental jubilee' (Michael Horovitz's phrase for the 1965 Albert Hall reading) is less likely to be repeated, and though Henri, McGough and Patten can still often command big turnouts for their frequent appearances, such poets of other persuasions as Ted Hughes, Thom Gunn (on his few returns to Britain), Seamus Heaney and Geoffrey Hill draw in even bigger ones on the rarer occasions they read in public. In other words, 'pop' is no longer wholly and specially popular.

16

Scotland, Wales, Ireland

Despite the fact of ease of communication in Britain today – or perhaps partly because of it – there are certain regions that seem very conscious of themselves as entities: the role played by Liverpool and the North-East in the pop movement was significant. But the Celtic awareness in Scotland, Wales and Northern Ireland has become even stronger during the present century, heightened in Ulster by the clash – the physical clash – between separate cultures. The expression of this has mainly been political, but there have been signs in the poetry of these countries too.

The so-called Scottish Renaissance has looked to the poet Hugh MacDiarmid at least as far back as the 1920s. His is still a potent and influential force, especially among those who have chosen to write in Lallans, the mixed literary-colloquial Scottish idiom which MacDiarmid did so much to promote. His *Complete Poems* were published in 1978. His more recent work was a prosy and sprawling attempt at epic form, parts of something called *The Kind of Poetry I Want,* and whatever importance he has lies in earlier work, written long before the period with which this essay deals. Many Scottish, and some other, critics would disagree, seeing in the whole body of his work, Scots and English, a deeply serious intellectual growth from national to international concerns. But it is the sometimes brisk, sometimes lyrical flavour of his early Scots poems that is more palpable to me.

MacDiarmid's Lallans lies behind almost everything that Sydney Goodsir Smith did, and some of Smith's lyrics (in his *Collected Poems,* 1975) are as attractive as his master's. Of all the poets writing in Lallans, the most entertaining was probably Robert Garioch, who died in 1980. Garioch was a comic observer of the Scottish scene, with a marvellous ear for the raciness of its speech:

> Last night in Scotland Street I met a man
> that gruppit my lapel – a kinna foreign
> cratur he seemed; he tellt me, There's a war on
> atween the Lang-nebs and the Big-heid Clan.

I wasna fasht, I took him for a moron,
naething byordnar, but he said, Ye're wan
of thae lang-nebbit folk, and if I can,
I'm gaunnae pash ye doun and rype your sporran.

('I'm Neutral')

But to an outsider, the best work now being done in Scotland is
written in English, particularly by Norman MacCraig, Ian Crichton
Smith and George Mackay Brown. MacCaig is an elegant, witty,
almost dandified poet, whose earlier poems were very polished and
exact. More recently he has been writing in a freer, more casual
manner, still alertly checking up on appearance and reality – his
habitual occupation – but without the trim trussing of rhyme that
used to give his fancies an aptness:

The sea is invisible
Under a sun-scatter of light.

What are you invisible under?
From what hard foreland of being
Do I fail to see you?

('Three Invisibles')

This looks rather lame and arbitrary compared with the fine
precision of these lines from an earlier poem, describing sheep which
have just been dipped:

They haul themselves ashore. With outraged cries
They waterfall uphill, spread out and stand
Dribbling salt water into flowers' eyes.

('Sheep Dipping')

But there is sometimes a compensating openness in the more
whimsical poems MacCaig has produced, and a refusal to be glib and
final:

> On the rug by the fire
> a stack of vocabulary rose up, confidently
> piling adjectives and nouns and
> tiny muscular verbs, storey by storey,
> till they reached
> almost to the ceiling. The word at the bottom
> was love.

> ('The Root of It')

Ian Crichton Smith has written in Gaelic as well as in English, but
his English poetry has no obvious verbal relationship with anything
Scottish. His themes, however, are very much of the remote
Scottish islands and highlands:

> if I shall say I had a jar it would
> be a black mountain in the Hebrides
>
> and round it fly your blackbirds black as pitch
> and in their centre with a holy book
>
> a woman all in black reading the world
> consisting of black crows in a black field.

> ('The Black Jar')

The pressure, momentum and craftsmanship of Smith's best poems
are impressive: everything is well shaped, strong, and there is often a
grim humour, contrasting Scotland's bloody and heroic past with
the diminished present, or looking sardonically at petty chauvinism
and the absurdities of cant about 'the quality of our civilization, our

language, and the perpetuation of our culture'. At the American nuclear site at Holy Loch he observes:

> The huge sea widens from us, mile on mile.
> Kenneth MacKellar sings from the domed pier.
> A tinker piper plays a ragged tune
> on ragged pipes. He tramps under a moon
> which rises like the dollar. Think how here
>
> missiles like sugar rocks are all incised
> with Alabaman Homer. These defend
> the clattering tills, the taxis, thin pale girls
> who wear at evening their Woolworth pearls
> and from dewed railings gaze at the world's end.
>
> ('Dunoon and the Holy Loch')★

Some of Smith's best poems are contained in the two sequences published together as *Love Poems and Elegies* (1972).

George Mackay Brown writes almost exclusively about his native Orkney, cold, rocky, depopulated, a place of shepherds, fishermen and memories of the distant Norse past of feud and destruction. It is a bleak existence, to which Brown gives grave and minute attention:

> What the women fold
> Are torn nets, a stretch of yarn from the loom,
> Sheaf after sheaf of August oats,
> In the cupboard cheese and honey and ale and bread,
> Shapes in the womb,
> Night long as a shroud when the twelve boats
> Are drifting lights in the west
> And the ebb ravels itself in rock and sand.
>
> ('Foldings')

Old legends, ballads, the grim inheritance of the Calvinist tradition and the louring menace of the weather are his material, handled with such suppleness that he is seldom monotonous. He is, in Scotland, a more varied and less forbidding equivalent in some ways to R.S. Thomas in Wales.

There seems to be no dominant figure among Anglo-Welsh poets today, though R.S. Thomas is the best-known and Dannie Abse is well respected. But many Anglo-Welsh writers themselves see a continuing flowering of Welsh poetry written in English, beginning with David Jones, going on through Dylan Thomas (who died in 1953), Vernon Watkins (died 1967) and Alun Lewis (died in Burma in 1944 at the age of twenty-nine), and present today in the work of Emyr Humphreys, Roland Mathias, John Ormond, John Tripp, Harri Webb, and such younger poets as Gillian Clarke and Robert Minhinnick.

One noticeable feature among several of the younger Anglo-Welsh poets is a vein of disillusion, even cynicism, about the very thing they are attempting to do. For example, John Davies has written a poem with the title 'How to Write Anglo-Welsh Poetry':

First, apologise for not being able
to speak Welsh. Go on: apologise.
Being Anglo-*any*thing is really tough;
any gaps you can fill with sighs.

And get some roots, juggle names like
Taliesin and ap Gwilym, weave
a Cymric web. It doesn't matter what
they wrote. Look, let's not be naive.

Now you can go on about the past
being more real than the present –
you've read your early R.S. Thomas,
you know where Welsh Wales went.

Spray place-names around. Caernarfon.
Cwmtwrch. Have, perhaps, a Swansea

sun marooned in Glamorgan's troubled
skies; even the weather's Welsh, see . . .

('How to Write Anglo-Welsh Poetry')

The dominance of Yeats, and to a much smaller extent of Patrick
Kavanagh, in Irish poetry seems to have left an eloquent legacy to
their present-day descendants, and there survives in Ulster a
devotion to 'the well-made verse' which is often lacking in England.
Thomas Kinsella during the 1950s began to publish poems that were
both sinewy and mellifluous, and he has been followed in the North
by Seamus Heaney, Michael Longley, Derek Mahon, Paul
Muldoon, and others. Kinsella's superb lyrical gift, shown in such
poems as 'Laundress' (from *Downstream,* 1962), extended itself to
longer elegiac and meditative pieces, in which there is intellectual
strenuousness but also a consummate descriptiveness:

Watcher in the tower, be with me now
At your parapet, above the glare of the lamps.
Turn your milky spectacles on the sea
Unblinking; cock your ear.

A rich darkness
Alive with signals: lights flash and wink;
Little bells clonk in the channel near the rocks;
Howth twinkles across the bay; ship-lights move
By invisible sea-lanes; the Baily light
Flickers, as it sweeps the middle darkness,
On some commotion . . .

('Nightwalker')

'Love, death and the artistic act' are Kinsella's stated themes, and like
most of his Irish contemporaries and juniors he refuses to be
deflected into either propaganda or the easy blandishments of pop
poetry: his stance, and theirs, is dignified, confident, basically
traditional but flexible too. Richard Murphy's long poems, such as

'The Last Galway Hooker' and 'The Battle of Aughrim', are also meditative, but less highly wrought than Kinsella's: they consider Irish history and his own roots in the west of Ireland, and have a refined and simple solidity.

I have already mentioned Seamus Heaney as one of a number of poets whose earlier work seems to have been affected by the 'Nature Poetry' of Ted Hughes's first two books; but it would be very inaccurate, as well as very unfair, to leave the matter like that. Heaney's books have been better received than all but a few during the time since the appearance of the first of them, *Death of a Naturalist* (1966). What has been noticed has been his verbal and physical precision, fresh eyes and fresh phrases:

> As a child, they could not keep me from wells
> And old pumps with buckets and windlasses.
> I loved the dark drop, the trapped sky, the smells
> Of waterweed, fungus and dank moss.

> ('Personal Helicon')

Death of a Naturalist was full of the personal, sensuous remembrance of things past, drawing on Heaney's own childhood in rural Derry. With *Door Into the Dark* (1969) he began to move beyond himself, looking for example at 'the mysterious life-cycle of the eel and the compulsive work-cycles in the eel-fisherman's life' in 'A Lough Neagh Sequence'. In *Wintering Out* (1972) he began to make a journey he was to repeat, back into the remote past, of Ireland and of prehistoric man:

> We picked flints,
> Pale and dirt-veined,

> So small finger and thumb
> Ached around them;

Cold beads of history and home
We fingered, a cave-mouth flame

Of leaf and stick
Trembling at the mind's wick.

('Tinder')

All these manoeuvres, both of extending his subject-matter beyond
rural simplicities and of tightening up his style so that it became an
economical and refined reduction to essentials, reached their
maturity in *North* (1975). In the words of the publisher's blurb to this
book: 'Here the Irish experience is refracted through images drawn
from different parts of the Northern European experience, and the
idea of the north allows the poet to contemplate the violence on his
home ground in relation to memories of the Scandinavian and
English invasions which have marked Irish history so indelibly.' The
message was one of continuity, established right from the beginning
in the two dedicatory poems (seed cutters who 'compose the frieze/
With all of us there, our anonymities' are the subject of the second of
these), and going on through the bog corpses, the Viking invaders,
the English massacres, an English journalist in search of 'views/On
the Irish thing', to the 'inner emigré' the poet sees himself as having
become, 'a wood-kerne/Escaped from the massacre.' Digging back
– and a kind of delicate linguistic excavation is the method of much
of Heaney's more recent poetry – he found tangled continuities in the
whole matter of Ireland:

I push back
through dictions,
Elizabethan canopies
Norman devices,

the erotic mayflowers
of Provence
and the ivied latins
of churchmen

to the scop's
twang, the iron
flash of consonants
cleaving the line.

('Bone Dreams')

The poems that drew their inspiration from the prehistoric bog
corpses of Scandinavia and Ireland found grimmer continuities than
those of language, as in 'Punishment', in which the execution of an
Iron Age girl for adultery is seen as analogous to the ritualistic
punishment of women, presumed traitors, in Northern Ireland,
who have been shaved and tarred by extremists as an 'example' to
others. The poet is torn between the force of 'connive' and the force
of 'understand':

My poor scapegoat,
I almost love you
but would have cast, I know,
the stones of silence.
I am the artful voyeur

of your brain's exposed
and darkened combs,
your muscles' webbing
and all your numbered bones:

I who have stood dumb
when your betraying sisters,
cauled in tar,
wept by the railings,

who would connive
in civilized outrage
yet understand the exact
and tribal, intimate revenge.

('Punishment')

Seamus Heaney
(Photograph Fay Godwin)

Heaney's recent book, *Field Work* (1979), is a further extension of these attempted acts of understanding and reconciliation, and uses a continuing metaphor of his withdrawal for a time to the rural depths of Southern Ireland, for example in 'The Harvest Bow':

> *The end of art is peace*
> Could be the motto of this frail device
> That I have pinned up on our deal dresser –
> Like a drawn snare
> Slipped lately by the spirit of the corn
> Yet burnished by its passage, and still warm.

> ('The Harvest Bow')

Heaney has had much more attention and praise than any other Ulster poet, and both are deserved. But an almost inevitable concomitant has been that other gifted poets from the province have suffered from comparative neglect. Among them is Michael Longley, a Protestant by background, who in verse letters to his Roman Catholic friend Heaney and to his fellow Protestant Derek Mahon has expressed with sinewy intelligence the conflicts of their embattled homeland. In his letter to Heaney, Longley recollects 'the old stories':

> The midden of cracked hurley sticks
> Tied to recall the crucifix,
> Of broken bones and lost scruples,
> The blackened hearth, the blazing gable's
> Telltale cinder where we may
> Scorch our shins until that day
> We sleepwalk through a No Man's Land
> Lipreading to an Orange band.

> ('Letter to Seamus Heaney')

And in a companion letter to Mahon:

> And did we come into our own
> When, minus muse and lexicon,
> We traced in August sixty-nine
> Our imaginary Peace Line
> Around the burnt-out houses of
> The Catholics we'd scarcely loved,
> Two Sisyphuses come to budge
> The sticks and stones of an old grudge,
>
> Two poetic conservatives
> In the city of guns and long knives,
> Our ears receiving then and there
> The stereophonic nightmare
> Of The Shankill and The Falls,
> Our matches struck on crumbling walls
> To light us as we moved at last
> Through the back alleys of Belfast?
>
> ('Letter to Derek Mahon')

But Longley is by no means solely a political poet. There is an elegant exactness about things seen in his poems, as in 'Thaw'*:

> Snow curls into the coalhouse, flecks the coal.
> We burn the snow as well in bad weather
> As though to spring-clean that darkening hole.
> The thaw's a blackbird with one white feather.

His recent book, *The Echo Gate* (1979), which includes 'Thaw', is full of precise and suggestive poems: the burden of several of them is the inter-penetration of things, the responsibility of one thing for another, best seen perhaps in 'The Linen Industry', a marvellous extended metaphor, or in 'Self-portrait', a truly witty poem which ends:

> I am, you will have noticed, all fingers and thumbs
> But, then, so is the wing of a bat, a bird's wing.
> I articulate through the nightingale's throat,
> Sing with the vocal chords of the orang-outang.

Derek Mahon is equally adept as a technician, with an ironical air which is sometimes almost dandified:

> Somewhere beyond the scorched gable end and the
> > burnt-out buses
> > there is a poet indulging
> > > his wretched rage for order –
> > or not as the case may be; for his
> > > is a dying art,
> > > an eddy of semantic scruples
> > > in an unstructurable sea.
>
> ('Rage for Order')

If his talent is occasionally in danger of thinning itself away into arbitrariness and whimsy, Mahon has shown at least once that he can indeed manage something more solid: his book *The Snow Party* (1975) ends with a most impressive poem, a meditation with the bleak title 'A Disused Shed in Co. Wexford'. Here 'A thousand mushrooms crowd to a keyhole', and are celebrated as dumb survivors whose tenacity spells out a hard-won lesson:

> They are begging us, you see, in their wordless way,
> To do something, to speak on their behalf
> Or at least not to close the door again.
> Lost people of Treblinka and Pompeii!

'Save us, save us', they seem to say,
Let the god not abandon us
Who have come so far in darkness and in pain.
We too had our lives to live.
You with your light meter and relaxed itinerary,
Let not our naive labours have been in vain!

('A Disused Shed in Co. Wexford')

Paul Muldoon emerged very young with his first book, *New Weather* (1973), published when he was only 21. His authority has increased with succeeding books, particularly in the poem that dominates *Why Brownlee Left* (1980), 'Immram'. This is a serio-comic mini-epic, in which the poet discovers his legendary ancestor Mael Duin, in terms of a strange mixture of tough Americanese and deliberately outrageous Irish blarney. But Muldoon works on a smaller scale with equal assurance:

The Volkswagen parked in the gap,
But gently ticking over.
You wonder if it's lovers
And not men hurrying back
Across two fields and a river.

('Ireland')★

Other Northern Irish poets of considerable accomplishment are Frank Ormsby, Tom Paulin, William Peskett and James Simmons. The most recent to make an impact has been Medbh McGuckian: in 1979 she won first prize in the National Poetry Competition with a poem, 'The Flitting', which is mysteriously, richly thick with metaphor.

17

Tony Harrison and Douglas Dunn

Two poets who first began to be known and praised about fifteen
years ago have by now become widely recognized as among the
finest poets of the middle generation: Tony Harrison and Douglas
Dunn. They came from working-class backgrounds (Harrison in
Leeds, Dunn in Scotland), have continued to live their adult lives
away from the metropolis (Harrison in Newcastle, Dunn in Hull),
and these facts have had a strong bearing on their poetry.

Tony Harrison's first full-length book, *The Loiners* (1970), is full
of highly wrought poems, dense, strenuous, laced with proper
names. He has worked in Nigeria and has travelled widely
elsewhere, and there are comic as well as pungent exoticisms in his
apostrophe to 'The White Queen':

> Professor! Poet! Provincial Dadaist!
> Pathic, pathetic, half-blind and half-pissed
> Most of these tours in Africa. A Corydon
> Past fifty, fat, these suave looks gone,
> That sallow cheek, that young Novello sheen
> gone matt and puffed. A radiant white queen
> In sub-Saharan scrub I hold my court
> On expat pay, my courtiers all bought.

One of the longest poems in *The Loiners,* 'Newcastle is Peru', takes
its title from the 17th-century poet John Cleveland, and there is
something of Cleveland's manner in Harrison's congested, fantastic,
occasionally over-ingenious dazzling flights. Harrison's poems are
constantly aware of ironies and oppositions, not least in his wry,
sometimes bitter recognition of his own cleverness and eloquence set
against a traditionally dour and reticent working-class Yorkshire
upbringing:

Tony Harrison
(Photograph Michael Mayhew)

How you became a poet's a mystery!
Wherever did you get your talent from?

I say, I had two uncles, Joe and Harry –
one was a stammerer, the other dumb.

('Heredity')★

This is the prefatory poem to *The School of Eloquence* (1978). The
poems in the title-sequence, further expanded and added to in
Continuous (1981), are Harrison's central achievement in coming to
terms with society, class and language. They are written in
compactly rhyming sixteen-line 'sonnets', and are by turns
contemptuous, nostalgic, acid, affectionate: they juxtapose
Yorkshire dialect and Yorkshire speech with semantic and
lexicographical learning, and show the same pertinacious and
entertaining brilliance Harrison has brought to his widely performed
translations of Molière, Racine and Aeschylus. Other poems in these
books look more directly and personally, and more movingly, at
family lives and family deaths, as in the poem on his mother's
cremation:

Gold survives the fire that's hot enough
to make you ashes in a standard urn.
An envelope of coarse official buff
contains your wedding ring which wouldn't burn.

Dad told me I'd to tell them at St. James's
that the ring should go in the incinerator.
That 'eternity' inscribed with both their names is
his surety that they'd be together, 'later'.

I signed for the parcelled clothing as the son,
this cardy, apron, pants, bra, dress –

the clerk phoned down: *6-8-8-3-1 ?*
Has she still her ring on? (slight pause) *Yes!*

It's on my warm palm now, your burnished ring!
I feel your ashes, head, arms, breasts, womb, legs,
sift through its circle slowly, like that thing
you used to let me watch to time the eggs.

('Timer')★

Douglas Dunn's *Terry Street* (1969) took as its base a poor working-
class part of Hull, a city which has appeared in some of Philip
Larkin's poems too; but Dunn's are quite different in spirit and
construction, lacking the finished and final quality of Larkin.
Instead, they have a guarded quirkiness, an obliqueness, a hesitant
cadence all his own, as in 'A Removal from Terry Street'★:

On a squeaking cart, they push the usual stuff,
A mattress, bed ends, cups, carpets, chairs,
Four paperback westerns. Two whistling youths
In surplus US Army battle-jackets
Remove their sister's goods. Her husband
Follows, carrying on his shoulders the son
Whose mischief we are glad to see removed,
And pushing, of all things, a lawnmower.
There is no grass in Terry Street. The worms
Come up cracks in concrete yards in moonlight.
That man, I wish him well, I wish him grass.

There may seem an artlessness about this observation, but it is
deceptive in its slow, circumstantial rumination. Elsewhere in the
book Dunn produced more bravura performances, such as the
grotesque 'A Poem in Praise of the British'; and he went on in his
next two books, *The Happier Life* (1972) and *Love or Nothing* (1974),
to a wider variety of more complex things, not always with total
conviction. It was with *Barbarians* (1979) that Dunn began to explore
imaginatively something more congenial: he attempted to
rediscover and repossess his own native country, Scotland, in terms
both of class and of nationhood. This reached its finest form,

technically and in feeling, in *St Kilda's Parliament* (1981), his best
book so far. Among the considerable variety of this book, one of the
most directly moving poems is the most personal, 'Washing the
Coins', a childhood memory of lifting potatoes, among casual
workers who were mostly Irish, of being mistaken for an Irish boy,
and of being apologized to for the mistake:

> She knew me, but she couldn't tell my face
> From an Irish boy's, and she apologized
> And roughed my hair as into my cupped hands
> She poured a dozen pennies of the realm
> And placed two florins there, then cupped her hands
> Around my hands, like praying together.
> It is not good to feel you have no future.
> My clotted hands turned coins to muddy copper.
> I tumbled all my coins upon our table.
> My mother ran a basin of hot water.
> We bathed my wages and we scrubbed them clean.
> Once all that sediment was washed away,
> That residue of field caked on my money,
> I filled the basin to its brim with cold;
> And when the water settled I could see
> Two English kings among their drowned Britannias.
>
> ('Washing the Coins')

Against the nostalgias and elegiac lamentations that perhaps
dominate *St Kilda's Parliament* should be weighed much good
humour about, and straightforward pleasure in, the things of this
world, and a spacious range of other feelings – wry, indignant,
ribald, sly, affectionate.

18

New poets since 1970:
James Fenton, Craig Raine,
Christopher Reid, Kit Wright,
Peter Reading, John Whitworth,
Peter Scupham, John Mole,
George Szirtes, Andrew Motion,
Michael Hulse

The best new poets who have come forward since about 1970, now mostly in their early thirties, seem to owe little direct allegiance to the dominant poets of the Fifties and Sixties, Philip Larkin and Ted Hughes, and none at all to the 'pop' poets. The first, and still the most intellectually a audacious, was James Fenton. His *Terminal Moraine* (1972) showed him as in some ways an heir of the games-playing Auden, but in no obvious sense. His 'Open Letter to Richard Crossman' is brilliant Byronic-Audenesque political and literary satire, and the book also contains bits of riddling rococo (such as 'The Kingfisher's Boxing Gloves'), 'Our Western Furniture', which is a long and formal sequence of poems about the opening-up of Japan to the West, and much else, including 'The Pitt-Rivers Museum, Oxford', which looks at this 'vast gymnasium or barracks' and finds in its clutter of dusty, bizarre and frightening objects a warning:

> Go
> As a historian of ideas or a sex-offender,
> For the primitive art,
> As a dusty semiologist, equipped to unravel
> The seven components of that witch's curse
> Or the syntax of the mutilated teeth. Go

In groups to giggle at curious finds.
But do not step into the kingdom of your promises
To yourself, like a child entering the forbidden
Woods of his lonely playtime.

After that book's publication, Fenton's activities as a political
journalist and as a foreign correspondent (in South-East Asia and
Germany) seemed for some years to distract him from poetry. A few
poems appeared in periodicals or in small pamphlets, but it was not
until his *The Memory of War* (1982), a collected volume that took in
much of *Terminal Moraine* and many later poems, that it could be
seen how his varied experiences, at home and abroad, had borne
fruit. The same sharp intelligence that was apparent in the first book
is there, but without the smart tricks. 'A German Requiem' has a
proverbial plainness, confronting guilt and the aftermath of war:

His wife nods, and a secret smile,
Like a breeze with enough strength to carry one dry leaf
Over two pavingstones, passes from chair to chair.
Even the enquirer is charmed.
He forgets to pursue the point.
It is not what he wants to know.
It is what he wants not to know.
It is not what they say.
It is what they do not say.

'Found poetry' and 'curious lore' are still Fenton's sources, but he has
matured in such a way that he is no longer simply an entertainer
(though he is that too) but a wise and weighty blender of disparate
elements.

In some influential quarters, the poetry of Craig Raine has been
welcomed as 'one of the most arresting debuts for a decade', 'one of
the most distinctive voices to have emerged in the past few years'.
These words of praise were for *The Onion, Memory* (1978), which
has been followed by *A Martian Sends a Postcard Home* (1979) and a
smaller collection, *A Free Translation* (1981). Raine is a poet who

James Fenton
(Photograph Laurence Burns)

works almost entirely in highly figurative invention, with metaphors and similes deployed ingeniously over ordinary things so that they become extraordinary. In the title-poem of the second book, for example, everyday objects are presented as bizarre discoveries, as if for the first time:

> Caxtons are mechanical birds with many wings
> and some are treasured for their markings –
>
> they cause the eyes to melt
> or the body to shriek without pain.
>
> I have never seen one fly, but
> sometimes they perch on the hand.

James Fenton has written of Raine that he has 'taught us to become strangers in our familiar world, to release the faculty of perception and allow it to graze at liberty in the field of experience'. One can accept the ingenuity, be amused by the originality of likenesses; but, granted this and the confident phrase-making skill, there can be uneasiness – even boredom – at what becomes too much like a repeated party trick. Raine tends to write in flatly declarative unrhymed couplets which, if not actually rhythmically inert, have small sense of forward movement: one thing after another.

In this, he is less sprightly than a poet who has been closely linked with him, Christopher Reid. Reid's *Arcadia* (1979) and *Pea Soup* (1982) have the same pert inquisitiveness and comic metaphorical talent, but these are harnessed to almost equally playful measures – for example, pigs' heads on the counter of a butcher's shop:

> With ears like wings, these pallid putti –
> hideous symbols of eternal beauty –
>
> relax on parsley and smirk about
> their newly-disembodied state.

('H. Vernon')

The influence of Raine and Reid has been rapid and widespread, noticeable in many poets both younger and older in the past few years. My refusal to be utterly impressed must be balanced against the rapture and hyperboles with which they have been received.

A more straightforwardly comic poet, with a marked rhythmical energy, is Kit Wright. He has written much very funny verse for young children, and his two full-length collections for adults, *The Bear Looked Over the Mountain* (1977) and *Bump-Starting the Hearse* (1983), have an exuberance which is infectious. As Roger Garfitt has pointed out, 'He has something of the music-hall approach of the Liverpool poets, but is quite distinct from them in his integrity of feeling and in his formal skill'. At least once – in 'Versions of Dr Tyerley – he brings his light touch to bear on a grimmer subject.

Grim humour has increasingly become Peter Reading's trademark – something which would not have been guessed from his first book, *For the Municipality's Elderly* (1974), a collection which was full of sensitivity and observation but which tended towards the solemn. Since then Reading has been both prolific (five more books, the most recent *Diplopic* in 1983) and sardonically disconcerting, finding material for poems in the oddest places. His reports on madness, obsession and cruelty, and on the vagaries and absurdities of love and sex, come from an imagination that is as sharp as it is bizarre; and he writes in a great variety of forms. Both he and John Whitworth have probably learned a lot from Gavin Ewart's poems, in their openness before the distinctions of 'good taste' and 'bad taste', their formal variety, and their humour. John Whitworth has published two books, *Unhistorical Fragments* (1980) and *Poor Butterflies* (1982), both of them ribald, rueful views of *l'homme moyen sensuel* in the later twentieth century. School, university, pubs, hotels, suburban backwaters, are frequent settings, and the speakers are brash, nostalgic, foul-mouthed, and without many illusions.

Three poets of a more deliberate weightiness who can be considered together are Peter Scupham, John Mole and George Szirtes. Scupham is the oldest, not publishing his first full-length collection (*The Snowing Globe*, 1972) until he was almost forty. His scrupulous, measured language is much concerned with survivals and continuities, with mortality and buried experience, and it is organized with a lavish but extremely disciplined care, well exemplified in his sonnet-sequence which gives the title to *The*

Hinterland (1977) – fifteen poems dexterously woven together into a tapestry, the theme of which is the First World War. John Mole is a more glancing, elusive writer, these qualities appropriately tied to the mystery and fragility of the habitual. His book *Feeding the Lake* (1981) contains some memorable lyrical pieces, such as 'The Skill'*:

What's left but the skill?
I float on a rhyme
And am half asleep.
Though these waters shine
They are not still
Nor do they run deep.

You have taken the sense
From all that I seemed to know –
Soon, on a dry bed,
I shall dream the slow
Deceptive confluence
By which our lake was fed.

George Szirtes (who came to England as a small boy after the 1956 Hungarian uprising) trained as a painter and graphic artist, and he has an acute visual perception in his shaping of a seen world, juxtaposing details with both clarity and mystery, as in

I say there will be hopelessness before
The children rise and the chair topples back:
The bright, transparent skins will fold and crack
Before the painter leaves by the back door.

('Group Portrait with Pets')

Two young poets who have written with a strong sense of historical perspective, who also share themes of exile, but who formally are quite distinct, are Andrew Motion and Michael Hulse. A melancholy ache of loss permeates Motion's work, and this can become monotonous rather than moving in his only full-length book so far, *The Pleasure Steamers* (1978); but since that book he has produced more vivid work, for example in the fragmentary narrative 'Independence', which had separate publication in 1981. Here the story of a man long retired from India to England is told obliquely, in his own words but less circumstantially than would be likely in a conventional dramatic monologue. Michael Hulse's allegiances are more European (he taught for several years in German universities), and he writes as a kind of metaphysical outsider, most memorably in the painful 'Twentieth Burning in the Bishopric of Wurzburg', included in his *Knowing and Forgetting* (1981).

19

'The Poetry Business'

An acute young poet, critic and editor, Blake Morrison in 1981 published an essay on 'Poetry and the Poetry Business' which attempted to look at the economics of poetry in Britain today in relation to the poetry that is actually produced: that is, whether there is a connection between the publishing, distribution, reviewing, buying and reading of poetry and the 'restraints and limitations that have been felt to mar contemporary English poetry'. It is a well-informed piece of good-tempered polemic, and makes some very sharp – and sometimes very true – comments. There is no doubt that the brief poetry 'boom' of the 1960s (about which I wrote in the 1973 version of my present essay – I now see with unfounded optimism) is over, and probably largely for economic reasons. Penguin Books have cut off their regular Penguin Modern Poet series, and their 'King Penguin' poets are more sporadic. Most commercial publishers (with the notable exceptions of Faber, Chatto & Windus, Oxford University Press, and Secker & Warburg) have totally abandoned any policy of having a poetry list; though there has been the brave rise of the Carcanet New Press during the past ten years, concentrating on poetry, and on such a scale that it can hardly any longer be considered a 'small press'; and more recently the Salamander Press in Edinburgh has produced books that are 'fine' in both a critical and bibliophile sense. The weeklies and monthlies (*The Times Literary Supplement*, the *New Statesman*, the *Listener*, *Encounter* and the *London Magazine*, augmented now by the fortnightly *London Review of Books*) do continue to publish poems regularly, but the 'little' magazines – given wholly or almost wholly to poetry – of which I wrote towards the end of 1972 have suffered in the bleak economic climate. Nevertheless, many come and go, and some persist.

There have been some shifts in other directions, however. 'But there is no competition', wrote T.S. Eliot in 'East Coker'. Poetry in the 1980s seems to have overtaken this statement, at least in a literal sense. Certainly the most publicized phenomenon in recent years has been the poetry competition, sometimes on a very grand scale. The organization known as the Arvon Foundation, which runs courses for amateur writers ('tutored' by professionals) in its centres in Yorkshire and Devon, has combined with a television company, the *Observer* newspaper and Sotheby's, the art-dealers, to mount competitions for unpublished poems: a major prize of £5,000 and many smaller prizes, which attract as many as 40,000 entries, each entrant paying a small fee for each poem, a method which itself pays for the scheme. The National Poetry Society, in conjunction with the BBC's 'serious' radio network, Radio 3, has run similar annual competitions with slightly smaller prizes (and, it would seem as a result, slightly fewer entries). Literary festivals associated with such places as Cheltenham, Lancaster and other centres have gone in for the same sort of activity.

The value, and even the seemliness, of such contests has been questioned. Are they vulgar lotteries, inimical to true poets? Some have said so. But the fact remains that poets with genuine gifts have more often than not been prizewinners in these competitions – most of which insist on anonymous or pseudonymous entries, so that no one can be accused of favouritism: poets such as Craig Raine, Andrew Motion, Tony Harrison, Michael Hulse, Hugo Williams, U.A. Fanthorpe and Medbh McGuckian, all mentioned elsewhere in this survey, have been major prizewinners in one competition or another during the past few years. And it seems true that, in an even-handed way, some of these poets have had their reputations confirmed and extended by such public successes (Harrison, Motion, Raine, Williams) and others have to some extent been actually 'discovered' (Hulse, McGuckian). Distinguished poets, and poets of very various persuasions, have taken on the job of judging: Larkin, Causley, Ted Hughes, Heaney, Barker, Spender, Mitchell, MacBeth, McGough, Dunn, and a whole roll-call of others. Whether one likes it or not, the competition – or lottery – is at present unignorable.

In a less glamorous but arguably more solid way, the activities of the Poetry Book Society, founded in 1954 by a board of directors which included T.S. Eliot, have helped to improve the chronic economic difficulties of poets and their publishers. Each year the Society makes four 'Choices' and a number of 'Recommendations'. A chosen book will have a guaranteed sale to members of the P.B.S., and this amounts to almost exactly a thousand copies. Therefore a publisher, told beforehand that one of his books is a P.B.S. 'Choice', can – without taking undue risks – print something more like 2,000 copies rather than 750 or 800: and the benefit reaches the poet (in practical terms as well as those of prestige) in addition to the publisher. These figures may seem absurdly small when compared with the print-runs and sales of new poetry books one hears about in Eastern Europe and China. But it is, to be realistic, an open, competitive market, and not something rigged by ideological supervisors. And though sales of 2,000 copies are considered very good in the British poetry market, a few poets do considerably better than that: apart from the continuing popularity of John Betjeman, there are such sales as those of Philip Larkin (70,000 of *The Whitsun Weddings*), Ted Hughes (50,000 of *Crow*), and Seamus Heaney (30,000 of *North*). The joint paperback selection of Thom Gunn and Ted Hughes which Faber astutely published, in view of the extent to which Gunn and Hughes are taught together on school and university syllabuses, has (according to Blake Morrison) now sold well over 100,000 copies. That at least some good new poetry, whether or not under an educational blanket, is reaching so many people is not to be sneered at.

Select Bibliography

The poet's birth-date follows the name.
When a poet has produced a comprehensive volume of Collected (or sometimes Selected) Poems, details of earlier volumes have been on the whole omitted.

ABSE, Dannie (1923–)
Collected Poems 1948–1976 (Hutchinson, 1977). *Way Out in the Centre* (Hutchinson, 1981).

ADCOCK, Fleur (1934–)
Tigers (OUP, 1967). *High Tide in the Garden* (OUP, 1971). *The Scenic Route* (OUP, 1974). *The Inner Harbour* (OUP, 1979). *Selected Poems* (OUP, 1983).

ALVAREZ, A. (1929–)
Autumn to Autumn and Selected Poems 1953–1976 (Macmillan, 1978).

AMIS, Kingsley (1922–)
Collected Poems 1944–1979 (Hutchinson, 1979).

AUDEN, W.H. (1907–73)
Collected Poems (Faber, 1976).

BARKER, George (1913–)
Collected Poems 1930–1955 (Faber, 1957). *The View of a Blind I* (Faber, 1962). *Dreams of a Summer Night* (Faber, 1966). *The Golden Chains* (Faber, 1968). *Poems of Places and People* (Faber, 1971). *In Memory of David Archer* (Faber, 1973).

Dialogues Etc. (Faber, 1976). *Villa Stellar* (Faber, 1978). *Anno Domini* (Faber, 1983).

BEER, Patricia (1924–)
Selected Poems (Hutchinson, 1979:). *The Lie of the Land* (Hutchinson, 1983).

BETJEMAN, John (1906–84)
Collected Poems (Murray, 1958; rev. 1979). *Summoned by Bells* (Murray, 1960). *Uncollected Poems* (Murray, 1982).

BROCK, Edwin (1927–)
Song of the Battery Hen – Selected Poems 1959–1975 (Secker & Warburg, 1977). *The River and the Train* (Secker & Warburg, 1979).

BROWN, George Mackay (1921–)
Selected Poems (Hogarth Press, 1977).

BROWNJOHN, Alan (1931–)
Collected Poems 1952–83 (Secker & Warburg, 1983).

BUNTING, Basil (1900–)
Collected Poems (OUP, 1978).

CAUSLEY, Charles (1917–)
Collected Poems 1951–1975 (Macmillan, 1975).

CLARKE, Gillian (1937–)
The Sundial (Gomer, 1978). *Letter*

133

from a Far Country (Carcanet New Press, 1982).

COBBING, Bob (1920–)
Cygnet Ring: Collected Poems Volume One (Tapocketa Press, 1977). *ABC/ Wan Do Tree: Collected Poems Volume Two* (El Uel Uel U Publications, 1978). *A Peal in Air: Collected Poems Volume Three 1968– 1970* (Phenomena Press, 1978). *The Kollekted Kris Kringle: Collected Poems Volume iv* (Anarcho Press, 1979).

CONQUEST, Robert (1917–)
Poems (Macmillan, 1955). *Between Mars and Venus* (Hutchinson, 1962). *Arias from a Love Opera and Other Poems* (Macmillan, 1969). *Forays* (Hogarth Press, 1979).

DAVIE, Donald (1922–)
Collected Poems 1950–1970 (Routledge & Kegan Paul, 1972). *Collected Poems 1970–1983* (Carcanet New Press, 1983).

DAVIES, John (1944–)
At the Edge of the Town (Gomer, 1981). *The Silence in the Park* (Poetry Wales Press, 1982).

DAY LEWIS, C. (1904–72)
Poems 1925–1972 (Cape, Hogarth Press, 1977).

DOWNIE, Freda (1929–)
A Stranger Here (Secker & Warburg, 1977). *Plainsong* (Secker & Warburg, 1981).

DUNN, Douglas (1942–)
Terry Street (Faber, 1969). *The Happier Life* (Faber, 1972). *Love or Nothing* (Faber, 1974). *Barbarians* (Faber, 1979). *St Kilda's Parliament* (Faber, 1981).

DURRELL, Lawrence (1912–)
Collected Poems 1931–1974 (Faber, 1980).

ELIOT, T.S. (1888–1965)
The Complete Poems and Plays (Faber, 1969).

EMPSON, William (1906–84)
Collected Poems (Chatto & Windus, 1955).

ENRIGHT D.J. (1920–)
Collected Poems (OUP, 1981).

EWART, Gavin (1916–)
The Collected Ewart 1933–1980 (Hutchinson, 1980). *The New Ewart: Poems 1980–1982* (Hutchinson, 1982).

FANTHORPE, U.A. (1929–)
Side Effects (Harry Chambers/Peterloo Poets, 1978). *Standing To* (Harry Chambers/Peterloo Poets, 1982).

FEAVER, Vicki (1943–)
Close Relatives (Secker & Warburg, 1981).

FENTON, James (1949–)
Terminal Moraine (Secker &

Warburg, 1972). *The Memory of War: Poems 1968–1982* (Salamander Press, 1982). *The Memory of War and Children in Exile* (Penguin, 1983).

FISHER, Roy (1930–)
Poems 1955–1980 (OUP, 1980).

FULLER, John (1937–)
Fairground Music (Hogarth Press, 1961). *The Tree that Walked* (Hogarth Press, 1967). *Cannibals and Missionaries* (Secker & Warburg, 1972). *Epistles to Several Persons* (Secker & Warburg, 1973). *The Mountain in the Sea* (Secker & Warburg, 1975). *Lies and Secrets* (Secker & Warburg, 1979). *The Illusionists: A Tale* (Secker and Warburg, 1980). *The Beautiful Inventions* (Secker & Warburg, 1983).

FULLER, Roy (1912–)
Collected Poems 1936–1961 (Deutsch, 1962). *Buff* (Deutsch, 1965). *New Poems* (Deutsch, 1968). *Tiny Tears* (Deutsch, 1973). *From the Joke Shop* (Deutsch, 1975). *The Reign of Sparrows* (London Magazine Editions, 1980).

GARIOCH, Robert (1909–80)
Collected Poems (Macdonald, 1983).

GASCOYNE, David (1916–)
Collected Poems (OUP, 1965). *The Sun at Midnight* (Enitharmon Press, 1970).

GRAHAM, Henry (1930–)
Good Luck to You Kafka, You'll Need it Boss (Rapp & Whiting, 1969). *Passport to Earth* (Rapp & Whiting, 1971). *Europe After Rain* (Headland Publications, 1981).

GRAHAM, W.S. (1918–)
Collected Poems 1942–1977 (Faber, 1979).

GRAVES, Robert (1895–)
Collected Poems 1975 (Cassell, 1975).

GRIGSON, Geoffrey (1905–)
Collected Poems 1924–1962 (Phoenix House, 1963). *The Cornish Dancer and Other Poems* (Secker & Warburg, 1982). *Collected Poems 1963–1980* (Allison & Busby, 1982). *Montaigne's Tower* (Secker & Warburg, 1984).

GUNN, Thom (1929–)
Fighting Terms (Fantasy Press, 1954; rev. Faber, 1962). *The Sense of Movement* (Faber, 1957). *My Sad Captains and Other Poems* (Faber, 1961). *Touch* (Faber, 1967). *Moly* (Faber, 1971). *Jack Straw's Castle* (Faber, 1976). *The Passages of Joy* (Faber, 1982).

HAMBURGER, Michael (1924–)
Collected Poems (Carcanet New Press, 1984).

HAMILTON, Ian (1938–)
The Visit (Faber, 1970).

HARRISON, Tony (1937–)

The Loiners (London Magazine Editions, 1970). *From the School of Eloquence and Other Poems* (Collings, 1978). *Continuous: 50 Sonnets from the School of Eloquence* (Collings, 1981).

HARSENT, David (1942–)
A Violent Country (OUP, 1969). *After Dark* (OUP, 1973).

HEANEY, Seamus (1939–)
Death of a Naturalist (Faber, 1966). *Door into the Dark* (Faber, 1969). *Wintering Out* (Faber, 1972). *North* (Faber, 1975). *Field Work* (Faber, 1979).

HENRI, Adrian (1932–)
The Best of Henri: Selected Poems 1960–1970 (Cape, 1975), *Guy Hedges: Poems 1970–1976* (Cape, 1977). *Penny Arcade* (Cape, 1983).

HILL, Geoffrey (1932–)
For the Unfallen: Poems 1952–1958 (Deutsch, 1959). *King Log* (Deutsch, 1968). *Mercian Hymns* (Deutsch, 1971). *Tenebrae* (Deutsch, 1978). *The Mystery of the Charity of Charles Péguy* (Deutsch/Agenda, 1983).

HOBSBAUM, Philip (1923–)
The Place's Fault and Other Poems (Macmillan, 1964). *In Retreat and Other Poems* (Macmillan, 1966). *Coming Out Fighting* (Macmillan, 1969). *Women and Animals* (Macmillan, 1972).

HOLBROOK, David (1923–).
Imaginings (Putnam, 1961). *Against*

the Cruel Frost (Putnam, 1963). *Object Relations* (Methuen, 1967). *Old World New World* (Rapp & Whiting, 1969). *Chance of a Lifetime* (Anvil Press Poetry, Collings, 1978).

HOROVITZ, Michael (1935–)
Declaration (New Departures, 1963). *Bank Holiday* (Latimer Press, 1967). *Love Poems* (New Departures, 1971). *The Wolverhampton Wanderer* (Latimer, New Dimensions Ltd for Poetry United, 1971). *Growing Up: Selected Poems and Pictures, 1951–1979* (Allison & Busby, 1979).

HUGHES, Glyn (1935–)
Neighbours: Poems 1965–1969 (Macmillan, 1970). *Rest the Poor Struggler: Poems 1969–1971* (Macmillan, 1972). *Alibis and Convictions* (Ceolfrith Press, 1978). *Best of Neighbours: New and Selected Poems* (Ceolfrith Press, 1979).

HUGHES, Ted (1930–)
The Hawk in the Rain (Faber, 1957). *Lupercal* (Faber, 1960). *Wodwo* (Faber, 1967). *Crow* (Faber, 1970). *Season Songs* (Faber, 1976). *Gaudete* (Faber, 1977). *Cave Birds* (Faber, 1978). *Remains of Elmet: A Pennine Sequence* (Faber, 1979). *Moortown* (Faber, 1979). *Selected Poems 1957– 1981* (Faber, 1982). *River* (Faber, 1983).

HULSE, Michael (1955–)
Knowing and Forgetting (Secker & Warburg, 1981).

HUMPHREYS, Emyr (1919–)
Ancestor Worship (Gwasg Gee, 1970).

JAMES, Clive (1939–)
Peregrine Prykke's Pilgrimage through the London Literary World (Cape, 1976). *The Fate of Felicity Fark in the Land of the Media* (Cape, 1975). *Britannia Bright's Bewilderment in the Wilderness of Westminster* (Cape, 1976). *Fan-Mail: Seven Verse Letters* (Faber, 1977). *Charles Charming's Challenges on the Pathway to the Throne* (Cape, 1981).

JENNINGS, Elizabeth (1926–)
Collected Poems (Macmillan, 1967). *The Animals' Arrival* (Macmillan, 1969). *Lucidities* (Macmillan, 1970). *Relationships* (Macmillan, 1972). *Growing Points* (Carcanet New Press, 1975). *Consequently I Rejoice* (Carcanet New Press, 1977). *Moments of Grace* (Carcanet New Press, 1979). *Celebrations and Elegies* (Carcanet New Press, 1982).

JONES, Brian (1938–)
Poems (London Magazine Editions, 1966). *A Family Album* (London Magazine Editions, 1968). *Interior* (Ross, 1969). *For Mad Mary* (London Magazine Editions, 1974). *The Island Normal* (Carcanet New Press, 1980).

JONES, David (1895–1974).
In Parenthesis (Faber, 1937). *The Anathemata* (Faber, 1952). *The Tribune's Visitation* (Fulcrum Press, 1969). *The Sleeping Lord and Other Fragments* (Faber, 1974). *The*

Kensington Mass (Agenda Editions, 1975).

JOSEPH, Jenny (1932–)
The Unlooked-for Season (Scorpion Press, 1960). *Rose in the Afternoon and Other Poems* (Dent, 1974). *The Thinking Heart* (Secker & Warburg, 1978). *Beyond Descartes* (Secker & Warburg, 1983).

KINSELLA, Thomas (1928–)
Poems 1956–1973 (Dolmen Press, 1980).

LARKIN, Philip (1922–)
The North Ship (Fortune Press, 1945; rev. Faber, 1966). *The Less Deceived* (Marvell Press, 1955). *The Whitsun Weddings* (Faber, 1964). *High Windows* (Faber, 1974).

LERNER, Laurence (1925–)
Domestic Interior and Other Poems (Hutchinson, 1959). *The Directions of Memory: Poems 1958–1962* (Hogarth Press, 1963). *Selves* (Routledge & Kegan Paul, 1969). *A.R.T.H.U.R., The Life and Opinions of a Digital Computer* (Harvester Press, 1974). *The Man I Killed* (Secker & Warburg, 1980). *A.R.T.H.U.R. and M.A.R.T.H.A.: Or the Loves of the Computers* (Secker & Warburg, 1980). *Selected Poems* (Secker & Warburg, 1984). *Chapter and Verse* (Secker & Warburg, 1984).

LOGUE, Christopher (1926–)
Songs (Hutchinson, 1959). *Patrocleia*

(Scorpion Press, 1962). *Logue's A.B.C.* (Scorpion Press, 1966). *Pax* (Rapp & Carroll, 1967). *New Numbers* (Cape, 1969). *War Music* (Cape, 1981). *Ode to the Dodo* (Cape, 1981).

LONGLEY, Michael (1939–   )
No Continuing City: Poems 1963–1968 (Gill & Macmillan, 1969). *An Exploded View: Poems 1968–1972* (Gollancz, 1973). *Man Lying on a Wall: Poems 1972–1975* (Gollancz, 1976). *The Echo Gate: Poems, 1975–1979* (Secker & Warburg, 1979).

LUCIE-SMITH, Edward (1933–   )
A Tropical Childhood and Other Poems (OUP, 1961). *Confessions and Histories* (OUP, 1964). *Towards Silence* (OUP, 1968). *The Well-Wishers* (OUP, 1974)

MacBETH, George (1932–   )
Collected Poems 1958–1970 (Macmillan, 1971). *The Orlando Poems* (Macmillan, 1971). *Shrapnel* (Macmillan, 1973). *A Poet's Year* (Gollancz, 1973). *In the Hours Waiting for the Blood to Come* (Gollancz, 1975). *Buying a Heart* (Omphalos Press, J-Jay Publications, 1978). *Poems of Love and Death* (Secker & Warburg, 1980). *Poems from Oby* (Secker & Warburg, 1982). *The Long Darkness* (Secker & Warburg, 1983).

MacCAIG, Norman (1910–   )
Selected Poems (Hogarth, 1971). *The White Bird* (Chatto & Windus, 1973).

The World's Room (Chatto & Windus, 1974). *Old Maps and New: Selected Poems* (Hogarth Press, 1978). *The Equal Skies* (Hogarth Press, 1980). *A World of Difference* (Chatto & Windus, 1983).

MacDIARMID, Hugh (1892–1978)
Complete Poems 1920–1976 (Martin Brian & O'Keeffe, 1978).

McGOUGH, Roger (1937–   )
Frinck and Summer with Monika (Joseph, 1967). *Watchwords* (Cape, 1969). *After the Merrymaking* (Cape, 1971). *Gig* (Cape, 1973). *In the Glassroom* (Cape, 1976). *Holiday on Death Row* (Cape, 1979). *Waving at Trains* (Cape, 1982).

McGUCKIAN, Medbh (1950–   )
The Flower Master (OUP, 1982).

MacNEICE, Louis (1907–63)
Collected Poems (Faber, 1966).

MAHON, Derek (1941–)
Poems 1962–1978 (OUP, 1979). *The Hunt by Night* (OUP, 1982).

MANGNALL, Jim (1930–   )
The Lionheart Letters (Driftwood Publications, 1972).

MASSINGHAM, Harold (1932–   )
Black Bull Guarding Apples (Longman, 1965). *Frost-gods* (Macmillan, 1971).

MATHIAS, Roland (1915–   )
Break in Harvest (Routledge, 1946). *The Flooded Valley* (Putnam, 1948). *The Roses of Tretower* (Dock Leaves Press, 1952). *Absalom in the Tree*

(Gomer, 1971). *Snipe's Castle* (Gomer, 1979). *Burning Brambles* (Gomer, 1983).

MIDDLETON, Christopher (1926–) *Torse 3: Poems 1949–1961* (Longman, 1962). *Nonsequences: Selfpoems* (Longman, 1965). *Our Flowers and Nice Bones* (Fulcrum Press, 1969). *The Lonely Suppers of W.V. Balloon* (Carcanet New Press, 1975). *Pataxanadu* (Carcanet New Press, 1977). *Carminalenia* (Carcanet New Press, 1980). *III Poems* (Carcanet New Press, 1983).

MINHINNICK, Robert (1952–) *A Thread in the Maze* (Davies, 1978). *Life Sentences* (Poetry Wales Press, 1983).

MITCHELL, Adrian (1932–) *Adrian Mitchell's Collected Poems 1953–79, For Beauty Douglas* (Allison & Busby, 1982).

MITCHELL, Elma (1919–) *The Poor Man in the Flesh* (Harry Chambers/Peterloo Poets, 1976). *The Human Cage* (Harry Chambers/Peterloo Poets, 1979). *Furnished Rooms* (Harry Chambers/Peterloo Poets, 1983).

MOLE, John (1941–) *The Love Horse* (E.J. Morten, 1973). *A Partial Light* (Dent, 1975). *Our Ship* (Secker & Warburg, 1977). *From the House Opposite* (Secker & Warburg, 1979). *Feeding the Lake* (Secker & Warburg, 1981). *In and Out of the Apple* (Secker & Warburg, 1984).

MORGAN, Edwin (1920–) *Poems of Thirty Years* (Carcanet New Press, 1982).

MORGAN, Pete (1939–) *The Grey Mare Being the Better Steed* (Secker & Warburg, 1973). *The Spring Collection* (Secker & Warburg, 1979). *A Winter Visitor* (Secker & Warburg, 1983).

MORRISON, Blake (1950–) *Dark Glasses* (Chatto & Windus, 1984).

MOTION, Andrew (1952–) *The Pleasure Steamers* (Carcanet New Press, 1978). *Independence* (Salamander Press, 1981). *Secret Narratives* (Salamander Press, 1983).

MULDOON, Paul (1951–) *New Weather* (Faber, 1973). *Mules* (Faber, 1977). *Why Brownlee Left* (Faber, 1980). *Quoof* (Faber, 1983).

MURPHY, Richard (1927–) *Sailing to an Island* (Faber, 1963). *The Battle of Aughrim; and The God Who Eats Corn* (Faber, 1968). *High Island* (Faber, 1974). *Selected Poems* (Faber, 1979).

NICHOLSON, Norman (1914–) *Five Rivers* (Faber, 1944). *Rock Face* (Faber, 1948). *The Pot Geranium* (Faber, 1954). *A Local Habitation*

(Faber, 1972). *Sea to the West* (Faber, 1981).

PRYNNE, J.H. (1936–)
Poems (Agneau 2, 1982).

ORMOND, John (1923–)
Requiem and Celebration (Davies, 1969). *Definition of a Waterfall* (OUP, 1973).

RAINE, Craig (1944–)
The Onion, Memory (OUP, 1978). *A Martian Sends a Postcard Home* (OUP, 1979). *A Free Translation* (Salamander Press, 1981). *Rich* (Faber, 1984).

ORMSBY, Frank (1947–)
A Store of Candles (OUP, 1977).

READING, Peter (1946–)
For the Municipality's Elderly (Secker & Warburg, 1974). *The Prison Cell & Barrel Mystery* (Secker & Warburg, 1976). *Nothing for Anyone* (Secker & Warburg, 1977). *Fiction* (Secker & Warburg, 1979). *Tom O'Bedlam's Beauties* (Secker & Warburg, 1981). *Diplopic* (Secker & Warburg, 1983).

PATTEN, Brian (1946–)
Little Johnny's Confession (Allen & Unwin, 1967). *Notes to the Hurrying Man* (Allen & Unwin, 1969). *The Irrelevant Song* (Allen & Unwin, 1971). *Vanishing Trick* (Allen & Unwin, 1976). *Grave Gossip* (Allen & Unwin, 1979).

PAULIN, Tom (1949–)
A State of Justice (Faber, 1977). *The Strange Museum* (Faber, 1980). *Liberty Tree* (Faber, 1983).

REDGROVE, Peter (1932–)
Sons of My Skin: Selected Poems 1954–1974 (Routledge & Kegan Paul, 1975). *From Every Chink of the Ark and Other New Poems* (Routledge & Kegan Paul, 1977). *The Weddings at Nether Powers and Other New Poems* (Routledge & Kegan Paul, 1979). *The Apple-Broadcast: and Other New Poems* (Routledge & Kegan Paul, 1981).

PESKETT, William (1952–)
The Nightowl's Dissection (Secker & Warburg, 1975). *Survivors* (Secker & Warburg, 1980).

PLATH, Sylvia (1932–63)
Collected Poems (Faber, 1981).

REEVES, James (1909–78)
Collected Poems 1929–1974 (Heinemann, 1974).

PLOMER, William (1903–73)
Collected Poems (Cape, 1973).

REID, Christopher (1950–)
Arcadia (OUP, 1979). *Pea Soup* (OUP, 1982).

PORTER, Peter (1929–)
Collected Poems (OUP, 1983). *Fast Forward* (OUP, 1984).

RUMENS, Carol (1943–)
A Strange Girl in Bright Colours
(Quartet Books, 1973). *Unplayed
Music* (Secker & Warburg, 1981).
Star Whisper (Secker & Warburg,
1983).

SCANNELL, Vernon (1922–)
New and Collected Poems 1950–1980
(Robson, 1980). *Winterlude* (Robson,
1982).

SCOVELL, E.J. (1907–)
The River Steamer and Other Poems
(Cresset Press, 1956). *The Space
Between* (Secker & Warburg, 1982).

SCUPHAM, Peter (1933–)
The Snowing Globe (E.J. Morten,
1972). *Prehistories* (OUP, 1975). *The
Hinterland* (OUP, 1977). *Summer
Palaces* (OUP, 1980). *Winter Quarters*
(OUP, 1983).

SILKIN, Jon (1930–)
Poems New and Selected (Chatto &
Windus, 1966). *The Kilhope Wheel*
(Mid-Northumberland Arts Group,
1971). *Amana Grass* (Hogarth Press,
1971). *The Principle of Water*
(Carcanet New Press, 1974). *The
Little Timekeeper* (Carcanet New
Press, 1976). *The Psalms with their
Spoils* (Routledge & Kegan Paul,
1980). *Selected Poems* (Routledge &
Kegan Paul, 1980).

SIMMONS, James (1933–)
The Selected James Simmons
(Blackstaff Press, 1978). *Constantly
Singing* (Blackstaff Press, 1980).

SMITH, Iain Crichton (1928–)
Selected Poems (Gollancz, 1970). *Love
Poems and Elegies* (Gollancz, 1972).
Hamlet in Autumn (Macdonald,
1972). *The Notebooks of Robinson
Crusoe and Other Poems* (Gollancz,
1975). *In the Middle* (Gollancz, 1977).
Selected Poems 1955–1980
(Macdonald, 1981).

SMITH, Ken (1938–)
*Poet Reclining: Selected Poems
1962–1980* (Bloodaxe, 1982).

SMITH, Stevie (1902–71)
Collected Poems (Allen Lane, 1975).

SMITH, Sydney Goodsir (1915–75)
Collected Poems 1941–75 (John
Calder, 1975).

SPENDER, Stephen (1909–)
Collected Poems 1928–53 (Faber,
1955). *The Generous Days* (Faber,
1971).

STALLWORTHY, Jon (1935–)
Root and Branch (Hogarth Press,
1969). *Hand in Hand* (Hogarth Press,
1974). *The Apple Barrel: Selected
Poems 1955–1963* (OUP, 1974). *A
Familiar Tree* (Chatto & Windus,
OUP, 1978).

SZIRTES, George (1948–)
The Slant Door (Secker & Warburg,
1979). *November and May* (Secker &
Warburg, 1981). *Short Wave* (Secker
& Warburg, 1983).

THOMAS, D.M. (1935–)
Selected Poems (Secker & Warburg, 1983).

THOMAS, R.S. (1913–)
Selected Poems 1946–1968 (Hart-Davis, MacGibbon, 1973). *H'm* (Macmillan, 1972). *Laboratories of the Spirit* (Macmillan, 1975). *Frequencies* (Macmillan, 1978). *Between Here and Now* (Macmillan, 1981). *Later Poems* (Macmillan, 1983).

THWAITE, Anthony (1930–)
Poems 1953–1983 (Secker & Warburg, 1984).

TOMLINSON, Charles (1927–)
Selected Poems 1951–1974 (OUP, 1978). *The Shaft* (OUP, 1978). *The Flood* (OUP, 1981) *Notes from New York* (OUP, 1984).

TRIPP, John (1927–)
Collected Poems 1958–78 (Davies, 1978).

WAIN, John (1925–)
Poems 1949–1979 (Macmillan, 1980).

WALKER, Ted (1934–)
Fox on a Barn Door: Poems 1963–1964 (Cape, 1965). *The Solitaries: Poems 1964–1965* (Cape, 1967). *The Night Bathers: Poems 1966–1968* (Cape, 1970). *Gloves to the Hangman: Poems 1969–1972* (Cape, 1973). *Burning the Ivy: Poems 1976–1977* (Cape, 1978).

WEBB, Harri (1920–)
The Green Desert (Gomer, 1969). *A Crown for Branwen* (Gomer, 1974). *Rampage and Revel* (Gomer, 1977).

WEVILL, David (1935–)
Birth of a Shark (Macmillan, 1964). *A Christ of the Ice-Floes* (Macmillan, 1966). *Firebreak* (Macmillan, 1971). *Where the Arrow Falls* (Macmillan, 1973).

WHITWORTH, John (1945–)
Unhistorical Fragments (Secker & Warburg, 1980). *Poor Butterflies* (Secker & Warburg, 1982).

WILLIAMS, Hugo (1942–)
Symptoms of Loss (OUP, 1965). *Sugar Daddy* (OUP, 1970). *Some Sweet Day* (OUP, 1975). *Love-Life* (Deutsch, 1979).

WRIGHT, Kit (1944–)
The Bear Looked Over the Mountain (Salamander Press, 1977). *Bump-Starting the Hearse* (Hutchinson, 1983).

YOUNG, Andrew (1885–1971)
Complete Poems (Secker & Warburg, 1974).

Anthologies

New Lines 1, ed. Robert Conquest (Macmillan, 1956).

Penguin Book of Contemporary Verse, 1918–60, ed. Kenneth Allott (Penguin, 1962).

New Lines 2: An Anthology, ed. Robert Conquest (Macmillan, 1963).

A Group Anthology, ed. Philip Hobsbaum and Edward Lucie-Smith (OUP, 1963).

The New Poetry, ed. A. Alvarez (Penguin, 1962; rev. 1966).

The Liverpool Scene, ed. Edward Lucie-Smith (Donald Carroll, 1967).

Children of Albion: Poetry of the Underground in Britain, ed. Michael Horovitz (Penguin, 1969).

British Poetry Since 1945, ed. Edward Lucie-Smith (Penguin, 1970).

The Oxford Book of Twentieth-Century English Verse, ed. Philip Larkin (OUP, 1973).

Cambridge Book of English Verse 1939–1975, ed. Alan Bold (CUP, 1976).

The Oxford Book of Contemporary Verse 1945–1980, ed. D.J. Enright (OUP, 1980).

Poetry 1945–1980, ed. John Mole and Anthony Thwaite (Longman, 1983).

The Penguin Book of Contemporary British Poetry, ed. Blake Morrison and Andrew Motion (Penguin, 1983).

Index

Abse, D., 52–3, 108
Adcock, F., 76, 78
Aeschylus, 120
Alvarez, A., 52, 56, 66, 97, 99
Amis, K., 5, 38, 43–4
Apollinaire, G., 94
Arp, J., 93
Attila the Stockbroker, 1, 101
Auden, W.H., 9, 12–16, 19, 25, 31, 35, 80, 123
Augustine, St, 59
Ayres, P., 1

Bach, J.S., 68
Bacon, F., 60
Baines, J., 1
Barker, G., 22–3, 131
Baskin, L., 60
Basho, 94
Baybars, T., 66
Beatles, The, 100
Beer, P., 53
Bell, M., 76
Betjeman, J., 7–11, 132
Blake, W., 25
Brecht, B., 100
Brock, E., 75–6
Brown, G.M., 105, 107–8
Brownjohn, A., 5, 66, 74–5, 95
Bunting, B., 82, 90–1
Byron, Lord, 123

Cage, J., 68
Campbell, R., 12
Causley, C., 25, 36–7, 131
Clark, J.C., 1, 101
Clarke, G., 108
Cleveland, J., 118
Cobbing, B., 94–5, 96
Cohen, L., 100
Colquhoun, R., 23
Conquest, R., 38, 44
Crashaw, R., 87

Creeley, R., 91

Dale, P., 97
Daniel, J., 95
Davie, D., 38, 46, 47–8
Davies, J., 108
Day Lewis, C., 12, 18–20, 21
Dickinson, E., 45
Dodds, E.R., 18
Dodsworth, M., 49
Donne, J., 49
Downie, F., 78–9
Dunn, D., 97, 118, 121–2, 131
Durrell, L., 24
Dylan, B., 100

Eliot, T.S., 3, 7, 23, 43, 56, 87, 130, 131
Empson, W., 46, 86, 99
Enright, D.J., 38, 46
Ewart, G., 25, 35–6, 127

Fanthorpe, U. A., 78, 79, 131
Feaver, V., 78, 79–80
Fenton, J., 13, 97, 123–4, 126
Finlay, I.H., 93
Fisher, R., 82, 91–2
Freud, S., 31
Frost, R., 19
Fuller, J., 13, 53, 54, 97
Fuller, R., 25, 29–31
Furnival, J., 93

Garfitt, R., 66, 70, 127
Garioch, R., 104–5
Gascoyne, D., 23
Godwin, F., 60
Goethe, J.W. von., 46
Graham, H., 95
Graham, W.S., 24
Graves, R., 3–5, 44
Grigson, G., 25, 28–9, 97
Gunn, T., 38, 46, 48–51, 103, 132

Hamilton, I., 38–40, 97–9
Hardy, B., 62
Hardy, T., 19
Harrison, T., 118–21, 131
Harsent, D., 97, 99
Harwood, L., 91
Heaney, S., 62, 63, 65, 103, 109, 110–14, 131, 132
Henri, A., 1, 101–3
Hill, G., 62, 82–8, 89, 103
Hobsbaum, P., 66, 76
Holbrook, D., 76
Homer, 100
Horovitz, M., 1, 102
Houédard, D.S., 93
Hughes, G., 63, 64–5
Hughes, T., 38, 56–62, 63, 65, 66, 71, 73, 103, 110, 123, 131, 132
Hulse, M., 128–9, 131
Humphreys, E., 108

James, C., 55, 97
Jandl, E., 94
Jennings, E., 38, 44–5
Johnson, L.K., 1, 101
Johnson, S., 47
Jones, B., 76
Jones, D., 5–6, 87, 108
Joseph, J., 76, 77, 78
Jung , C., 31

Kandinsky, W., 93
Kavanagh, P., 109
Keats, J., 72
King, H., 70
Kinsella, T., 109–10

Larkin, P., 9, 38–43, 56, 61, 65, 121, 123, 131, 132
Lawrence, D.H., 88
Lax, R., 94
Lerner, L., 53
Lewis, A., 109
Logue, C., 100
Longley, E., 97

Longley, M., 109, 114–16
Lucie-Smith, E., 52, 66, 76, 82, 87

MacBeth, G., 66, 70–3, 95, 131
MacCaig, N., 105–6
MacDiarmid, H., 104
McGough, R., 1, 101–3, 131
McGuckian, M., 117, 131
McKueh, R., 100
MacNeice, L., 12, 16–18, 23, 29
MacSweeney, B., 91
Mahon, D., 109, 114, 115, 116–17
Mangnall, J., 95
Martial, 68
Massingham, H., 63, 65
Mathias, R., 108
Meredith, G., 19
Mickiewicz, A., 47
Milligan, S., 1
Milton, J., 46
Minhinnick, R., 108
Minton, J., 23
Mitchell, A., 66, 100–1, 131
Mitchell, E., 78, 79
Mole, J., 127–8
Molière, 120
Moore, M., 49
Morgan, E., 93–4
Morgan, P., 102
Morrison, B., 38, 130, 132
Motion, A., 128–9, 131
Muldoon, P., 109, 117
Murphy, R., 109

Nash, O., 25, 35
Nicholson, N., 24

Olson, C., 91
Ormond, J., 108
Ormsby, F., 117

Pasternak, B., 48
Patten, B., 1, 101–3
Paulin, T., 117
Péguy, C., 88

Perse, St J., 87
Peskett, W., 117
Pickard, T., 91
Plath, S., 62–3
Plomer, W., 10–11
Porter, P., 66, 67, 96
Pound, E., 6, 90, 91
Prynne, J., 91
Pushkin, A., 54

Racine, J., 120
Raine, C., 124–7, 131
Raworth, T., 91
Reading, P., 127
Redgrove, P., 63, 66, 73–4
Reeves, J., 5
Reid, C., 126–7
Ricks, C., 85
Riddell, A., 93
Rousseau, J.J., 47
Rumens, C., 78, 79, 80

Scannell, V., 52, 53
Scarfe, F., 22
Scovell, E.J., 80–1
Scupham, P., 127
Shakespeare, W., 43
Silkin, J., 63, 82, 88–9
Simmons, J., 117
Sitwell, E., 3
Skelton, R., 12
Smith, I.C., 105, 106–7
Smith, S., 25–8

Smith, S.G., 104
Snyder, G., 50
Spender, S., 12, 20–1, 65, 131
Stallworthy, J., 76, 97
Stevens, W., 89
Stoppard, T., 55
Swift, J., 47
Szirtes, G., 127–8

Tennyson, A., 87
Thomas, D., 22, 56, 62, 108
Thomas, E., 64
Thomas, R.S., 25, 31–5, 108
Tomlinson, C., 82, 89–90, 91
Tripp, J., 108
Tzara, T., 93

Uccello, P., 79

Wain, J., 38, 46–7
Walker, T., 63, 64
Watkins, V., 109
Webb, H., 108
Wevill, D., 63, 64, 66
Whitworth, J., 127
Wildman, E., 93
Williams, H., 97, 99, 131
Williams, W.C., 49, 89, 91
Wordsworth, W., 24, 64
Wright, K., 127

Yeats, W.B., 43, 49, 109
Young, A., 64